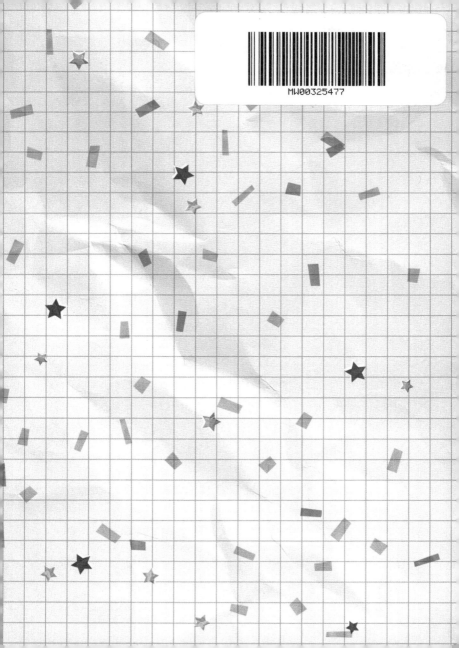

MW00325477

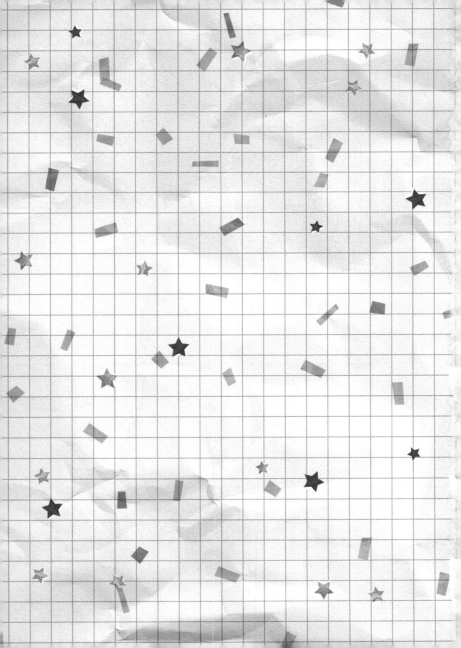

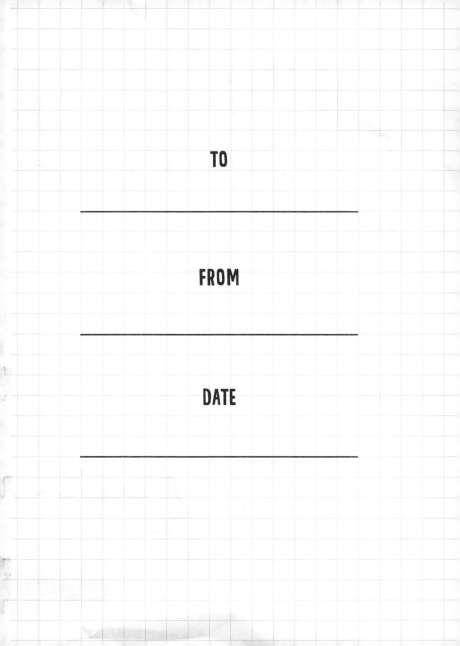

TO

_____

FROM

_____

DATE

_____

TOGETHER TIME

TIME

FUN-SIZED DEVOTIONS

FOR THE

WHOLE FAMILY

LIVE YOUR FAITH

Together Time: Fun-Sized Devotions for the Whole Family
Copyright © 2021 DaySpring Cards, Inc. All rights reserved.
First Edition, January 2021

Published by:

21154 Highway 16 East
Siloam Springs, AR 72761
dayspring.com

Written by: Lucy Schultz
Designed by: Hannah Skelton

Printed in China
Prime: J3102
ISBN: 978-1-64454-839-4

CONTENTS

1. Jesus Loves Us (Even When We Mess Up)................. 8
2. His Love Is Unfailing and Forgiving 10
3. God's Love Follows Through 12
4. The Storm (Don't Be Scared, God Protects Us!) 14
5. Don't Be Afraid! God Is in Charge..................... 16
6. Don't Be Afraid! There Is No Fear In Love 18
7. Lost Sheep (God Thinks We Are Valuable)...............20
8. Nothing Can Separate Us from God's Love 22
9. Godly Love.......................................24
Take 10!...26
10. Firm Foundation 28
11. Obedient and Disobedient Sons 30
12. Loving God First 32
13. Feed My Sheep....................................34
14. Treat Others How You'd Like to Be Treated 36
15. Servant Leaders...................................38
16. Fruit of the Gospel................................40
17. Good and Bad Fruit................................42
18. Fruit of the Spirit 44
Take 10!...46
19. Wonderfully Made.................................48
20. Here for a Reason 50
21. God Cares About Me 52
22. Adopted! (Gotcha Day) 54
23. Jesus Loves the Little Children 56
24. Family Matters....................................58
25. God-given Talents.................................60
26. Cheerful Giving 62
27. Opening the Door 64
Take 10!...66
28. Wisdom and Understanding 68
29. Truth and Honesty.................................70

30. A Guiding Light... 72
31. Shouts of Joy 74
32. Speak No Evil 76
33. Encouraging Words 78
34. Wisdom in Anger 80
35. Lazy Sloths.. 82
36. Love is Not Jealous 84
Take 10!... 86
37. Love Each Other 88
38. Help Is on the Way!.. 90
39. Help Is Here! 92
40. Ten Lepers 94
41. Thanks for Other Folks.................................... 96
42. Thanksgiving.. 98
43. Got Faith? Walking on Water 100
44. Got Faith? Jesus Heals the Crippled Man 102
45. Got Faith? Lazarus Lives................................. 104
Take 10!.. 106
46. Little Things, Huge Impacts............................... 108
47. Be a Giver, Not a Taker................................... 110
48. God Multiplies Generosity 112
49. Ask God 114
50. Ask and It Will Be Given 116
51. Say Again.. 118
52. Gifted and Talented 120
53. Exceptional Gifts.. 122
54. The Best Gift Is Free!...................................... 124
Take 10!.. 126
55. Victorious Power 128
56. Amazing Victory 130
57. Amazing God!.. 132
58. The Blind See! 134
59. A Change of Heart 136
60. Your Faith Made It Happen 138

61. Abundant Fishermen 140
62. Got Time for Food? 142
63. Freedom! 144
Take 10! 146
64. One God 148
65. Number One 150
66. One Way 152
67. Worship the Lord! 154
68. Praise the Lord! 156
69. Sing to the Lord! 158
70. Our Father 160
71. Pray for Whom? 162
72. He Hears Our Prayers 164
Take 10! 166
73. Which Way Is Right? 168
74. See the Light 170
75. Believing Hearts 172
76. Joy, Peace, and Patience 174
77. Rooted in Him 176
78. Love Like Jesus 178
79. Keep the Faith! 180
80. God's Awesome Power 182
81. God Never Leaves Us 184
Take 10! 186
82. He Brings Good News 188
83. Be My Proof 190
84. Sharing the Love 192
85. Calling Who? 194
86. To Do What? 196
87. What Else? 198
88. Standing Strong 200
89. Carry On 202
90. Time to Celebrate 204
Take 10! 206

1

JESUS LOVES US (EVEN WHEN WE MESS UP)

Jesus went on into Jericho and was passing through. There was a chief tax collector there named Zacchaeus, who was rich. He was trying to see who Jesus was, but he was a little man and could not see Jesus because of the crowd. So he ran ahead of the crowd and climbed a sycamore tree to see Jesus, who was going to pass that way. When Jesus came to that place, He looked up and said to Zacchaeus, "Hurry down, Zacchaeus, because I must stay in your house today."

Zacchaeus hurried down and welcomed Him with great joy. All the people who saw it started grumbling, "This man has gone as a guest to the home of a sinner!"

Zacchaeus stood up and said to the Lord, "Listen, sir! I will give half my belongings to the poor, and if I have cheated anyone, I will pay back four times as much."

Jesus said to him, "Salvation has come to this house today, for this man, also, is a descendant of Abraham. The Son of Man came to seek and to save the lost."

—Luke 19:1–10 GNT

LET'S THINK

Zacchaeus was a liar, a thief, and a cheat.
We've all done things that are wrong or that we're not proud of.
What are some things you "shoulda coulda" done differently?

...

Jesus wanted to go to Zacchaeus's house even though Zacchaeus was far from perfect. How do we know that He wants to be with us?

...

Zacchaeus wanted to pay people back and make things right.
Jesus did not require that. What can we do to show that we
love Jesus and want to make things right?

LET'S DO

Jesus loves us when we make good choices and when we make bad choices. Think about what you should apologize for—to God and to people. Once you say you're sorry, let go of it. Jesus is over it, and there's no need to feel bad about it again.
Share what you can do better.

LET'S PRAY

God, help us remember that Jesus loves us even when we mess up.
Thanks for loving us no matter what. In Jesus' name, amen.

2

HIS LOVE IS UNFAILING AND FORGIVING

The LORD is compassionate and merciful,
slow to get angry and filled with unfailing love.
He will not constantly accuse us,
nor remain angry forever.
He does not punish us for all our sins;
He does not deal harshly with us, as we deserve.
For His unfailing love toward those who fear Him
is as great as the height of the heavens above the earth.
He has removed our sins as far from us
as the east is from the west.
The LORD is like a father to His children,
tender and compassionate to those who fear Him.

—*Psalm 103:8–13 NLT*

LET'S THINK

The Bible tells us that the Lord is compassionate and merciful. Compassion is more than understanding someone's misery or bad situation; it's suffering with them. Compassion wants to lessen someone's pain and even go out of the way to do it. Mercy is similar but given by someone in power over another. It is greater kindness than one deserves, forgiveness, and a blessing. Mercy is something to be thankful for.

•••

Think in general and think specifically to yourself: What did God go out of His way to do? How has God blessed you with forgiveness?

•••

God, our heavenly Father, is the best. He is way better than our earthly fathers. Our dads mess up. Only our Heavenly Father is perfect.

LET'S DO

Think about God's compassionate desire to forgive and how it affects you. Share how you have seen or shown God's compassion or mercy to others. Our heavenly Father loves us so much. He is always there, ready to forgive!

LET'S PRAY

God, help us remember that You will never give up on us. Thanks for loving us through thick and thin. Thank You for forgiving us and treating us better than we deserve. Help us apologize and forgive with compassion the way You do. In Jesus' name, amen.

GOD'S LOVE FOLLOWS THROUGH

Give thanks to the LORD, for He is good! His faithful love endures forever.

—*Psalm 118:1 NLT*

Where is another God like you, who pardons the guilt of the remnant, overlooking the sins of His special people? You will not stay angry with Your people forever, because You delight in showing unfailing love. Once again You will have compassion on us. You will trample our sins under Your feet and throw them into the depths of the ocean! You will show us Your faithfulness and unfailing love as You promised to our ancestors Abraham and Jacob long ago.

—*Micah 7:18–20 NLT*

For this is how God loved the world: He gave His one and only Son, so that everyone who believes in Him will not perish but have eternal life. God sent His Son into the world not to judge the world, but to save the world through Him.

—*John 3:16–17 NLT*

LET'S THINK

The Bible tells us that God's unfailing love lasts forever.
Because of this, He will not stay angry. But what angers God?
Hint: He wants to trample them and throw them far away.
Why does He continue to forgive us? How did God show the world mercy?

•••

Compassion means being concerned for others in bad situations.
Sin is a bad situation to be in. How can we allow Jesus to fix it?

•••

The verses in Psalms and Micah come from the Old Testament.
They were written before Jesus was born. Think about how Jesus carried out
God's faithful promises even though He came years later.

LET'S DO

Think about the many times God has forgiven you or loved you
through a hard time. Is there someone you want or need to forgive?

•••

How can you share God's love this week?

•••

Later, if or when you need a reminder of God's unfailing, everlasting love, look
up Psalm 118:1–9, Daniel 9:4, Romans 15:4, and II Corinthians 1:20.

LET'S PRAY

God, help us remember that You always follow through because You are
faithful and forgiving. We are so grateful that You never will give up on
us. Thanks for loving us. In Jesus' name, amen.

THE STORM (DON'T BE SCARED, GOD PROTECTS US!)

Then He got into the boat and His disciples followed Him. Suddenly a furious storm came up on the lake, so that the waves swept over the boat. But Jesus was sleeping. The disciples went and woke Him, saying, "Lord, save us! We're going to drown!"

He replied, "You of little faith, why are you so afraid?" Then He got up and rebuked the winds and the waves, and it was completely calm.

The men were amazed and asked, "What kind of man is this? Even the winds and the waves obey Him!"

—*Matthew 8:23–27 NIV*

But even if we don't feel at ease, God is greater than our feelings, and He knows everything.

—*I John 3:20 CEV*

Our Lord, you bless those who live right,
and you shield them with your kindness.

—*Psalm 5:12 CEV*

In this story, Jesus and His friends, who were experienced fishermen, were in deep water in the middle of the lake when a huge storm blew in. The wind and waves were crazy, rocking the boat and tossing lots of water inside. His friends were terrified! And it seemed Jesus had no idea what was going on!

...

Jesus always knows what's going on. Have you had any scary experiences? How did He protect you?

LET'S DO

Think about a time when you were safe in God's arms. Share how God protects you.

...

Beginning in Acts 27, through Acts 28:10, you can read another really cool story about how God calmed the men facing a different storm. More mayhem followed but God protected them and was glorified— they realized how amazing God is.

LET'S PRAY

God, help us remember that You're always there when we are in trouble. Thanks for calming and protecting us during those times. In Jesus' name, amen.

5

DON'T BE AFRAID! GOD IS IN CHARGE.

God is our refuge and strength, a tested help in times of trouble. And so we need not fear even if the world blows up and the mountains crumble into the sea. Let the oceans roar and foam; let the mountains tremble!

There is a river of joy flowing through the city of our God—the sacred home of the God above all gods. God Himself is living in that city; therefore it stands unmoved despite the turmoil everywhere. He will not delay His help. The nations rant and rave in anger—but when God speaks, the earth melts in submission and kingdoms totter into ruin.

—Psalm 46:1–6 TLB

LET'S THINK

There are a lot of things in this world to be afraid of. Some people are afraid of heights or the dark; some are afraid of bees or snakes. But God tells us that we don't need to be afraid even if the world blows up and the mountains crumble into the sea!

•••

Who does the Bible say God is? What will God do in times of trouble? What will the earth do when God speaks?

•••

Many things can cause us to worry, stress, suffer, and feel helpless. But God will take care of us even in the most difficult and troublesome times.

LET'S DO

Take a minute to think about times you've been worried or scared—whether recently or whether they happened a long time ago. Take turns talking about them. What did you do, or what should you do, when scared?

•••

Now think about a time when you felt safe in God's arms. Tell about those.

•••

Pray together. Ask God for help in your specific situations and tell Him how grateful you are for His protection.

LET'S PRAY

God, help us remember that You are in charge and You are always there when we are scared. Thank You for being with us, helping us, and calming us. In Jesus' name, amen.

DON'T BE AFRAID! THERE IS NO FEAR IN LOVE

This is how God showed His love among us: He sent His one and only Son into the world that we might live through Him. This is love: not that we loved God, but that He loved us and sent His Son as an atoning sacrifice for our sins. . . . If anyone acknowledges that Jesus is the Son of God, God lives in them and they in God. . . .God is love. Whoever lives in love lives in God, and God in them. This is how love is made complete among us so that we will have confidence on the day of judgment: In this world we are like Jesus. There is no fear in love. But perfect love drives out fear, because fear has to do with punishment.

—I John 4:9–10, 15–18 NIV

LET'S THINK

God loves us so much that He sent His only Son into the world
to save us from our sins. When we disobey, we get in trouble with
people "in charge" like parents, teachers, bosses, and police.
But who is the One in charge of everything?

•••

What do today's verses say that God's love does?
Think about the bad things you have done and ask God
to forgive you. Thank Jesus for making it possible for you
to be saved and go to heaven someday.

LET'S DO

Talk to God. Tell Jesus how grateful you are for
His gift of salvation. Ask Him for the faith to know it's true.

•••

Share how God encourages you.

LET'S PRAY

God, help me remember what You did so that I don't have to be
afraid. Thank You for forgiving me. In Jesus' name, amen.

LOST SHEEP (GOD THINKS WE ARE VALUABLE)

Then Jesus told them this parable: "Suppose one of you has a hundred sheep and loses one of them. Doesn't he leave the ninety-nine in the open country and go after the lost sheep until he finds it? And when he finds it, he joyfully puts it on his shoulders and goes home. Then he calls his friends and neighbors together and says, 'Rejoice with me; I have found my lost sheep.' I tell you that in the same way there will be more rejoicing in heaven over one sinner who repents than over ninety-nine righteous persons who do not need to repent.

"Or suppose a woman has ten silver coins and loses one. Doesn't she light a lamp, sweep the house and search carefully until she finds it? And when she finds it, she calls her friends and neighbors together and says, 'Rejoice with me; I have found my lost coin.' In the same way, I tell you, there is rejoicing in the presence of the angels of God over one sinner who repents."

—Luke 15:3–10 NIV

LET'S THINK

The first parable is one of the reasons Jesus is called "The Good Shepherd." Jesus says that He is the Shepherd and we are lost sheep. What does a shepherd do? Why are we sheep?

...

The second parable compares us to lost coins. Coins are valuable. And a lost coin is worth looking for. What did Jesus do to show that He loves us? What can we do to make Jesus rejoice?

LET'S DO

In John 10:11–18, Jesus tells us that hired hands will run away from danger—but that the shepherd will die in order to protect his sheep. Jesus loves us so much that He died in order to save us. When we repent (when we say we are sorry for our sins) and then believe that Jesus took our punishment (by dying on the cross), we are no longer lost. We are found! Thank Jesus for loving you enough to find you and keep you safe. Share a time when you felt God close to you.

LET'S PRAY

God, help us remember that Jesus' love for us is so strong that He searches for us and carries us home. In Jesus' name, amen.

NOTHING CAN SEPARATE US FROM GOD'S LOVE

If God is for us, who can be against us? Certainly not God, who did not even keep back His own Son, but offered Him for us all! He gave us His Son—will He not also freely give us all things? . . . Who, then, can separate us from the love of Christ? Can trouble do it, or hardship or persecution or hunger or poverty or danger or death? . . . For I am certain that nothing can separate us from His love: neither death nor life, neither angels nor other heavenly rulers or powers, neither the present nor the future, neither the world above nor the world below—there is nothing in all creation that will ever be able to separate us from the love of God which is ours through Christ Jesus our Lord.

—Romans 8:31–32, 35, 38–39 GNT

Jesus left heaven when He came to earth to live and die for us. Dying for someone is the ultimate sacrifice that shows true love. God's love makes a way for us to not be separated from Him but to join Him in heaven someday!

...

God gives us so much and His love for us is so great that we can't begin to understand it. What else does God give us? What things does the Bible say we think can separate us from God? What did God give us as proof that He loves us? What did Jesus do to guarantee that love?

LET'S DO

The Bible tells us that sin (our disobedience) originally separates us from God. Take a minute to think. When we believe in His Son, Jesus, and accept His gift of grace, we are no longer separated. We are no longer enemies; we are friends!

...

Talk to God. Tell Jesus how grateful you are for His gift of love and grace. Ask Him for faith to not doubt it's true. And then share how God reminds you of His amazing love.

LET'S PRAY

God, help us remember that Jesus' love for us is bigger than we can imagine. Thank you, Jesus, for being our friend. In Jesus' name, amen.

GODLY LOVE

If I could speak all the languages of earth and of angels, but didn't love others, I would only be a noisy gong or a clanging cymbal. If I had the gift of prophecy, and if I understood all of God's secret plans and possessed all knowledge, and if I had such faith that I could move mountains, but didn't love others, I would be nothing. If I gave everything I have to the poor and even sacrificed my body, I could boast about it; but if I didn't love others, I would have gained nothing.

Love is patient and kind. Love is not jealous or boastful or proud or rude. It does not demand its own way. It is not irritable, and it keeps no record of being wronged. It does not rejoice about injustice but rejoices whenever the truth wins out. Love never gives up, never loses faith, is always hopeful, and endures through every circumstance.

—I Corinthians 13:1–7 NLT

Most importantly, love each other deeply. Love has a way of not looking at others' sins.

—1 Peter 4:8 ICB

LET'S THINK

The Bible tells us that we are nothing without God's love.
We could be famous, rich, or powerful—but all of those are worthless
if we don't have love. Why is love is so much more important?
Why does the rest "not count" if we don't have love?

...

Love is patient, kind, rejoices in right, always hopeful, and endures
forever. Who do you know has shown that kind of godly love?
How can they do it?

LET'S DO

Contemplate God's unfailing, everlasting love and how you
can show godly love to others. Pray silently and ask God to help
you love others the way Jesus does.

...

Share about godly love.

LET'S PRAY

God, help us to show godly love. Thank You for loving us
in the way only You can. In Jesus' name, amen.

TAKE TEN!

TAKE TURNS LETTING EACH FAMILY MEMBER ANSWER THE QUESTIONS BELOW.

About Family

1. What do you appreciate about yours?

2. What do you admire?

3. Why does God love them?

About You

4. When does God love you? Start with, "God loves me when I. . . ."

5. How many words can you come up with to describe God's love?

6 Can you think of one word to describe
   God's love for every letter in your name?

About Stuff

7 How do you like to celebrate
   Valentine's Day?

8 How many love songs can you and your
   family remember?

9 In what ways do you like people to show
   they love you?

10 What things do you love to do with
   your family?

FIRM FOUNDATION

So why do you keep calling Me "Lord, Lord!" when you don't do what I say? I will show you what it's like when someone comes to me, listens to My teaching, and then follows it. It is like a person building a house who digs deep and lays the foundation on solid rock. When the floodwaters rise and break against that house, it stands firm because it is well built. But anyone who hears and doesn't obey is like a person who builds a house right on the ground, without a foundation. When the floods sweep down against that house, it will collapse into a heap of ruins.

—*Luke 6:46–49 NLT*

If you love Me, keep my commands.

—*John 14:15 NIV*

LET'S THINK

Several places in the Bible, it says that if we love God, we will follow His rules and do what He says. Sometimes we listen and follow through with God's instructions and sometimes we don't. In the first passage, Jesus makes sure we understand how important it is to do as He says. He tells a story illustrating how we should respond to His instructions.

•••

Who is like a person building a house on a firm foundation?
Who is like a person building without a foundation?
Why do we need a firm foundation?

LET'S DO

The Bible is full of instructions. Did you know that all Ten Commandments are wrapped up in the Golden Rule— "Love your neighbor as you love yourself"?

•••

Jesus says that we show our love for Him when we love to do what He asks of us. How can you be a better "doer"?

LET'S PRAY

God, help us to listen and obey what You say.
Help us to do so because we love You and You love us.
Thanks for loving us by giving us Your Word. In Jesus' name, amen.

OBEDIENT AND DISOBEDIENT SONS

"Tell me what you think about this: There was a man who had two sons. He went to the first son and said, 'Son, go and work today in my vineyard.' The son answered, 'I will not go.' But later the son decided he should go, and he went. Then the father went to the other son and said, 'Son, go and work today in my vineyard.' The son answered, 'Yes, sir, I will go and work.' But he did not go. Which of the two sons obeyed his father?"

The priests and leaders answered, "The first son."

Jesus said to them, "I tell you the truth. The tax collectors and the prostitutes will enter the kingdom of God before you do. John came to show you the right way to live. And you did not believe him. But the tax collectors and prostitutes believed John. You saw this, but you still refused to change and believe him."

—*Matthew 21:28–32 ICB*

We show our love for God by obeying His commandments, and they are not hard to follow.

—*1 John 5:3 CEV*

LET'S THINK

Jesus tells a parable (a story) for us to think about. Do you think you are more like the first son or the second? What would your mom, dad, or someone else say about you? Why? What would help you do better?

•••

Think of some modern-day examples of kids asked to do something by their mother, father, grandparent, or teacher. Talk about it and make up your own parable that Jesus might tell to His disciples if they lived on earth today.

LET'S DO

Challenge #1: When someone tells you to do something this week, ask God to help you do it with a smile!

•••

Challenge #2: Surprise someone this week by doing a chore or something they'd like you to do—before they ask!

•••

Plan to share how God helped you do something you didn't want to do.

LET'S PRAY

God, help us obey You and follow through when others ask us for help. Help us to love others as You want us to. Thanks for helping us. In Jesus' name, amen.

LOVING GOD FIRST

I'd rather for you to be faithful and to know me
than to offer sacrifices.

—Hosea 6:6 CEV

But Samuel replied: "Does the LORD delight in burnt offerings
and sacrifices as much as in obeying the LORD? To obey is
better than sacrifice."

I Samuel 15:22 NIV

To love Him with all your heart, with all your understanding and
with all your strength, and to love your neighbor as yourself is more
important than all burnt offerings and sacrifices.

—Mark 12:33 NIV

Yet we know that a person is made right with God by faith in Jesus
Christ, not by obeying the law. And we have believed in Christ Jesus,
so that we might be made right with God because of our faith in
Christ, not because we have obeyed the law. For no one will ever be
made right with God by obeying the law.

—Galatians 2:16 NLT

LET'S THINK

*Do you know what a sacrifice is? Before Jesus was born,
God's people used to follow specific rules for worship.
Because they were constantly sinning, God required them to kill
special animals on certain days of each year in order to make things
right with Him. Often the people would still do whatever they
wanted—thinking that as long as they did their sacrifices when they
were supposed to, they were okay with God.*

...

*Why did God think they had an "attitude problem"?
What was His response?*

LET'S DO

Think about it. Talk about what Jesus' sacrifice means for us.

LET'S PRAY

*Thank You, God, for loving us even when we don't keep all the rules.
Help us to have the right heart attitude when we try.
In Jesus' name, amen.*

FEED MY SHEEP

I am the Good Shepherd. As the Father knows Me and I know the Father, in the same way I know my sheep and they know me. And I am willing to die for them.

—*John 10:14–15 GNT*

When they finished eating, Jesus said to Simon Peter, "Simon son of John do you love Me more than these?" He answered, "Yes, Lord, You know that I love You." Jesus said, "Take care of my lambs." Again Jesus said, "Simon son of John do you love Me?" He answered, "Yes, Lord, You know that I love You." Jesus said, "Take care of my sheep." A third time He said, "Simon son of John do you love Me?" Peter was hurt because Jesus asked him the third time, "Do you love Me?" Peter said, "Lord, You know everything. You know that I love You!" He said to him, "Take care of my sheep."

—*John 21:15–17 ICB*

I beg you to take care of God's flock, His people, that you are responsible for. Watch over it because you want to, not because you are forced to do it. That is how God wants it. Do it because you are happy to serve, not because you want money.

—*I Peter 5:1–2 ICB*

LET'S THINK

In John 10, Jesus calls Himself the Good Shepherd.
Who are His sheep? How do we know?

•••

Later, in John 21, Jesus asks Peter several times if he loves Him.
Since Peter does love Him, he should do as Jesus asks.
What do you suppose Jesus is asking Peter to do?

•••

If we love Jesus, should we take care of His sheep?
Peter writes to God's chosen people (Christians) who are scattered all
over the world to tell them to take care of God's sheep too.
What do you suppose that means?

LET'S DO

How can we care for and serve others? Talk about what each of you can
do. Brainstorm what you as a family can do to serve your community,
your neighborhood, and your own home.

•••

Plan to do something special for someone to show that you care.

LET'S PRAY

Thank You, God, for loving and caring for us. Help us show our love for
You by caring for and serving others as You do.
In Jesus' name, amen.

TREAT OTHERS HOW YOU'D LIKE TO BE TREATED

In the Law there are many commands, such as, "Be faithful in marriage. Do not murder. Do not steal. Do not want what belongs to others." But all of these are summed up in the command that says, "Love others as much as you love yourself."

—*Romans 13:9 CEV*

The second most important commandment says: "Love others as much as you love yourself." No other commandment is more important than these.

—*Mark 12:31 CEV*

All that the Law says can be summed up in the command to love others as much as you love yourself.

—*Galatians 5:14 CEV*

Treat others just as you want to be treated.

—*Luke 6:31 CEV*

LET'S THINK

The Bible tells us that the Ten Commandments are summed up in one: "Love others as much as you love yourself." It's easy to love ourselves. We were basically born thinking "Me first!"—but God tells us to put others first and treat them as we want to be treated. How do you like to be treated? How do you treat others in similar circumstances?

• • •

It's easy to think of how others "shoulda coulda" treated us nicer. But now is the time to think about you from their point of view. Put yourself in their shoes . . . first.

LET'S DO

Think about it. Before you do something your own way, think about another person and how they would want you to do it. Put yourself in their shoes and practice the Golden Rule. Ask God to help you.

• • •

Share about a time someone (or you) did the Golden Rule right.

LET'S PRAY

Thank You, God, for loving us and for teaching us to love others. Help us treat others as we'd like to be treated—or even better! In Jesus' name, amen.

SERVANT LEADERS

So Jesus called them together and said, "You know that the rulers in this world lord it over their people, and officials flaunt their authority over those under them. But among you it will be different. Whoever wants to be a leader among you must be your servant, and whoever wants to be first among you must be the slave of everyone else. For even the Son of Man came not to be served but to serve others and to give His life as a ransom for many."

—Mark 10:42–45 NLT

Now I tell you to love each other, as I have loved you. The greatest way to show love for friends is to die for them. And you are My friends, if you obey Me. Servants don't know what their master is doing, and so I don't speak to you as My servants. I speak to you as My friends, and I have told you everything that My Father has told me.

—John 15:12–15 CEV

LET'S THINK

All of us are leaders in some way even if we aren't official. We as leaders are called to be different. What should be different about us? What ways do you lead? We can literally die to save someone from danger. But for most people, that is not what Jesus asks us to do. He asks us to "die to self," which could be worded "live for others." What are some ways we can live for others?

LET'S DO

Lead by example this week. Work alongside someone and be a friend.

LET'S PRAY

Thank You, God, for loving us. Help us to lead others by serving them. Thank You for being our friend. In Jesus' name, amen.

FRUIT OF THE GOSPEL

You did not choose me. I chose you and sent you out to produce fruit, the kind of fruit that will last.

—John 15:16 CEV

A farmer went out to plant his seed. While he was planting, some seed fell beside the road. People walked on the seed, and the birds ate all this seed. Some seed fell on rock. It began to grow but then died because it had no water. Some seed fell among thorny weeds. This seed grew, but later the weeds choked the good plants. And some seed fell on good ground. This seed grew and made 100 times more grain . . .

"This is what the story means: The seed is God's teaching. What is the seed that fell beside the road? It is like the people who hear God's teaching, but then the devil comes and takes it away from their hearts . . . What is the seed that fell on rock? It is like those who hear God's teaching and accept it gladly. But . . . They stop believing and turn away from God. What is the seed that fell among the thorny weeds? It is like those who hear God's teaching, but they let the worries, riches, and pleasures of this life keep them from growing . . . And what is the seed that fell on the good ground? That is like those who hear God's teaching with a good, honest heart. They obey God's teaching and patiently produce good fruit.

—Luke 8:4–8, 11–15 ICB

LET'S THINK

As friends of Jesus, we are sent out to work alongside Him to produce eternal fruit. What is this fruit Jesus is talking about?

...

If God's Word (His teachings found in the Bible) grows in our hearts, we will produce good fruit. What can you do to know God's teachings?

LET'S DO

Challenge: Ask God to show you how He is using you to produce good fruit. Talk through those moments.

LET'S PRAY

Thank You, God, for loving us. Help us show our love for You by sharing Your Word with others. In Jesus' name, amen.

GOOD AND BAD FRUIT

Make a tree good and its fruit will be good, or make a tree bad and its fruit will be bad, for a tree is recognized by its fruit. . . A good man brings good things out of the good stored up in him, and an evil man brings evil things out of the evil stored up in him.

—*Matthew 12:33–35 NIV*

Be careful of false prophets. They come to you and look gentle like sheep. But they are really dangerous like wolves. You will know these people because of the things they do. Good things don't come from bad people, just as grapes don't come from thornbushes. And figs don't come from thorny weeds. In the same way, every good tree produces good fruit. And bad trees produce bad fruit. A good tree cannot produce bad fruit. And a bad tree cannot produce good fruit. Every tree that does not produce good fruit is cut down and thrown into the fire. You will know these false prophets by what they produce.

—*Matthew 7:15–20 ICB*

Even a child is known by his behavior. His actions show if he is innocent and good.

—*Proverbs 20:11 ICB*

LET'S THINK

Jesus compares good people with fruit trees and grapevines.
He compares evil people with thornbushes and weeds.
How do you know whose heart is good?
How can you tell whose heart is bad?

...

If someone does bad things, it doesn't make them a bad person.
Look at the whole picture. Good people still make mistakes and bad
people can do good things too. The Bible warns us of bad people
who look good. It's what's on the inside that counts.
What counts is their heart and love for God.

LET'S DO

The next time you hear, "Follow your heart,"
make sure your heart is in the right place.
Ask God to help you make the right choice.

LET'S PRAY

Thank You, God, for loving us. Help us make good choices.
In Jesus' name, amen.

18

FRUIT OF THE SPIRIT

So I command you to love each other.

—*John 15:17 CEV*

But the Spirit gives love, joy, peace, patience, kindness, goodness, faithfulness, gentleness, self-control. There is no law that says these things are wrong. Those who belong to Christ Jesus have crucified their own sinful selves. They have given up their old selfish feelings and the evil things they wanted to do. We get our new life from the Spirit. So we should follow the Spirit.

—*Galatians 5:22–25 ICB*

But the Helper will teach you everything. He will cause you to remember all the things I told you. This Helper is the Holy Spirit whom the Father will send in My name.

—*John 14:26 ICB*

LET'S THINK

God tells us that we must love each other. Paul wrote to the Galatians telling them that the Holy Spirit will help us love. God's Spirit gives us new life with new behavior! What other new feelings, behaviors, or fruit does the Holy Spirit give us? Think of a time when we need each of them.

...

Go through the list of what God's Spirit gives. Talk about what each one means. Focus on all the fruit as a whole. Don't focus on each individual behavior as things you need to work on. Ask God to use the Holy Spirit to work in you to show all of them more and more as you grow in Him.

LET'S DO

Talk about how the Holy Spirit is helping you be a better person.

LET'S PRAY

Thank You, God, for giving us a Helper to help us love and to remember everything Jesus tells us. Help us put the bad behind us and move forward with new life in Your Spirit. In Jesus' name, amen.

TAKE TEN!

TAKE TURNS LETTING EACH FAMILY MEMBER ANSWER THE QUESTIONS BELOW.

About Others

1. How can you show appreciation to someone who serves or served in the military?

2. If you were to be a caregiver, which ages would you like to work with and why?

3. Which career(s) do you think help a lot of people, and how?

About You

4. What kind of leader do you want to be?

5 Which two fruits are your favorites?
What about your least favorites?

6 What would you do differently if you were
in charge of _____?

About Stuff

7 How can people tell that you are happy?

8 How can people tell that you are sad?

9 How do you know the difference between
right and wrong?

10 How would life be different if you have to
eat only what you grow in your garden?

WONDERFULLY MADE

I praise You because You made me in an amazing and wonderful way. What You have done is wonderful. I know this very well. You saw my bones being formed as I took shape in my mother's body. When I was put together there, You saw my body as it was formed. All the days planned for me were written in Your book before I was one day old.

—*Psalm 139:14–16 ICB*

You have looked deep into my heart, LORD, and You know all about me. You know when I am resting or when I am working, and from heaven You discover my thoughts. You notice everything I do and everywhere I go. Before I even speak a word, You know what I will say, and with Your powerful arm You protect me from every side. I can't understand all of this! Such wonderful knowledge is far above me.

—*Psalm 139:1–6 CEV*

When birds are sold, two small birds cost only a penny. But not even one of the little birds can die without your Father's knowing it. God even knows how many hairs are on your head. So don't be afraid. You are worth much more than many birds.

—*Matthew 10:29–31 ICB*

LET'S THINK

There are so many, many people. How can God keep track of each one of us? David wonders this too! Somehow in God's infinite power, He knows us. When did God get to know you? What does God know about us? See if you can find all the ways David listed in the passages above. Hint: there are at least ten.

•••

Jesus tells us that we are more precious than a bunch of birds. That may not seem like much; lots of folk think people are better than birds. However, think about what He says: not one can die without your Father knowing about it.

LET'S DO

Talk about what you did today, knowing how much He cares about you. . . . Discuss what you suppose God was thinking—because He was looking!

•••

Tell someone something nice they did when they thought no one was looking. Brainstorm ways God made each of you special.

LET'S PRAY

Thank You, God, for knowing everything about each of us. Help us be assured that every one of us is precious to You. In Jesus' name, amen.

20

HERE FOR A REASON

But I have let you live for this reason: to show you My power. In this way My name will be talked about in all the earth.

—*Exodus 9:16 ICB*

Therefore, I urge you, brothers and sisters, in view of God's mercy, to offer your bodies as a living sacrifice, holy and pleasing to God—this is your true and proper worship.

—*Romans 12:1 NIV*

God has made us what we are. In Christ Jesus, God made us new people so that we would do good works. God had planned in advance those good works for us. He had planned for us to live our lives doing them.

—*Ephesians 2:10 ICB*

If anyone makes himself clean from evil things, he will be used for special purposes. He will be made holy, and the Master can use him. He will be ready to do any good work.

—*II Timothy 2:21 ICB*

Sometimes we wonder why we are here on this earth.
What is our purpose? God definitely has a purpose for each of us.
One main purpose is to glorify God. But what does that mean?
Think about how these Scriptures tell us we are useful to God.
Other than praise and worship, how does He use us to glorify Him?

...

We serve Him by living for Him rather than ourselves.
It's in His plan for us to do good things. Think about how to be ready,
to show, to serve, and to do what God wants.

LET'S DO

Talk about what good things you can do to glorify God—
today, this week, and this year.
Can you sing a song? Help others? Serve at church?

...

Be useful! God plans good things for you to do ahead of time,
and you can plan too. What will you be able to do in ten years
that you aren't able to do now?

LET'S PRAY

Thank You, God, for giving us a reason to live. Forgive us for our sins.
Help us be ready to do what You want us to do—and do it. In Jesus'
name, amen.

21

GOD CARES ABOUT ME

So Aaron spoke to the whole community of the Israelites. While he was speaking, they looked toward the desert. There the greatness of the Lord appeared in a cloud.

The Lord said to Moses, "I have heard the grumblings of the people of Israel. So tell them, 'At twilight you will eat meat. And every morning you will eat all the bread you want. Then you will know I am the Lord, your God.' "

That evening, quail came and covered the camp. And in the morning dew lay around the camp. When the dew was gone, thin flakes like frost were on the desert ground. When the Israelites saw it, they asked each other, "What is that?" They asked this question because they did not know what it was.

So Moses told them, "This is the bread the Lord has given you to eat. The Lord has commanded, 'Each one of you must gather what he needs. Gather about two quarts for every person in your family.' "

So the people of Israel did this. Some people gathered much, and some gathered little. Then they measured it. The person who gathered more did not have too much. The person who gathered less did not have too little. Each person gathered just as much as he needed.

—*Exodus 16:10–18 ICB*

LET'S THINK

God appeared in a cloud and spoke to His people when they felt "stranded" in the desert and were starving to death. God said He heard them! What did God hear them doing? What was God's solution? How soon did He provide for their needs?

...

Some people are actually starving and need food today. Others may need different things to survive. Maybe you need something as well. Paul tells us in Philippians 4:19 (NLT) that God will supply all our needs with the glorious riches of Jesus Christ! What do you and your family need?

LET'S DO

Talk more about those needs. As you have time, write them down, leaving space for the date that God answers them. Hebrews 11:1 (NIV) tells us this is faith: "confidence in what we hope for and assurance about what we do not see."

LET'S PRAY

Thank You, God, for caring for our needs. Help us trust that You will take care of all of them. In Jesus' name, amen.

22

ADOPTED! (GOTCHA DAY)

We know that in everything God works for the good of those who love Him. They are the people He called, because that was His plan. God knew them before He made the world, and He chose them to be like His Son so that Jesus would be the firstborn of many brothers and sisters. God planned for them to be like His Son; and those he planned to be like His Son, He also called; and those He called, He also made right with Him; and those He made right, He also glorified.

—Romans 8:28–30 NCV

Remember that in the past you were without Christ. You were not citizens of Israel, and you had no part in the agreements with the promise that God made to His people. You had no hope, and you did not know God. But now in Christ Jesus, you who were far away from God are brought near through the blood of Christ's death. . . . Now you who are not Jewish are not foreigners or strangers any longer, but are citizens together with God's holy people. You belong to God's family.

—Ephesians 2:12–13, 19 NCV

LET'S THINK

God had a plan before the world began—He knew all along that He would choose us to be in His family. Before Jesus came, the Jews (the Israelites) were God's chosen people. But God's love made a way for others to be adopted and part of God's family too!

...

How does it feel to know that God chose us?
What does it mean to be part of God's family?

LET'S DO

Talk about what it means to be adopted,
loved, and accepted in a family.

LET'S PRAY

Thank You, God, for adopting us into Your family.
Thanks for loving us like You love Your own Son.
In Jesus' name, amen.

23

JESUS LOVES THE LITTLE CHILDREN

Then the people brought their little children to Jesus so that He could put His hands on them and pray for them. When His followers saw this, they told the people to stop bringing their children to Jesus. But Jesus said, "Let the little children come to me. Don't stop them, because the kingdom of heaven belongs to people who are like these children." After Jesus put His hands on the children, He left there.

—Matthew 19:13–15 ICB

At that time the followers came to Jesus and asked, "Who is greatest in the kingdom of heaven?"

Jesus called a little child to Him. He stood the child before the followers. Then He said, "I tell you the truth. You must change and become like little children. If you don't do this, you will never enter the kingdom of heaven. The greatest person in the kingdom of heaven is the one who makes himself humble like this child.

"Whoever accepts a little child in My name accepts Me. If one of these little children believes in Me, and someone causes that child to sin, then it will be very bad for that person. It would be better for him to have a large stone tied around his neck and be drowned in the sea."

—Matthew 18:1–6 ICB

LET'S THINK

*From these verses, we know that Jesus loves children!
He doesn't want to see any of them pushed to the side or thought of as
less important. What do you think Jesus' followers were thinking when
they told the people to stop bugging Jesus?*

•••

*What do you think Jesus was talking to God about when He was
praying for the children? Humble means that you don't think you're
more important or more special than others. Jesus led by example.
Can you think of ways Jesus showed us how to be humble?*

LET'S DO

Talk and plan how to humbly serve others as Jesus did.

LET'S PRAY

*Thank You, God, for loving kids of all ages. Help us be humble like
children no matter how old we get. In Jesus' name, amen.*

24

FAMILY MATTERS

My true brother and sister and mother are those who do the things God wants.

—Mark 3:35 ICB

He purifies people from their sins, and both He and those who are made pure all have the same Father. That is why Jesus is not ashamed to call them His family.

—Hebrews 2:11 GNT

As I write this letter to you, I hope to come and see you soon. But if I delay, this letter will let you know how we should conduct ourselves in God's household [family], which is the church of the living God, the pillar and support of the truth. No one can deny how great is the secret of our religion: He appeared in human form, was shown to be right by the Spirit, and was seen by angels. He was preached among the nations, was believed in throughout the world, and was taken up to heaven.

—I Timothy 3:14–16 GNT

LET'S THINK

The Bible tells us that we can be in God's family.
What does Mark tells us is expected of members of God's family.

•••

In the letter to the Hebrews, what connects us all? How are we family?

•••

Paul's letter to Timothy tells us how Christians should behave since they are in God's family. He calls God's household or family "the church of the living God." Since he is not talking about an actual building, what is he talking about? What is the secret (or not-so-secret) mystery of our faith that holds us together as a family?

LET'S DO

Maybe your family has "house rules." Brainstorm rules for God's house that you can follow as members of God's family.

•••

Plan to share how you can do what God wants.

LET'S PRAY

Thank You, God, for making a way for us to be in Your family.
Help us behave in a way that pleases You as our heavenly Father.
In Jesus' name, amen.

25

GOD-GIVEN TALENTS

So [Jesus] said, "A nobleman went to a distant country to get royal power for himself and then return. He summoned ten of his slaves, and gave them [each one coin], and said to them, 'Do business with these until I come back.' But the citizens of his country hated him and sent a delegation after him, saying, 'We do not want this man to rule over us.' When he returned, having received royal power, he ordered these slaves, to whom he had given the money, to be summoned so that he might find out what they had gained by trading. The first came forward and said, 'Lord, your [coin] has made ten more [coins].' He said to him, 'Well done, good slave! Because you have been trustworthy in a very small thing, take charge of ten cities.' Then the second came, saying, 'Lord, your [coin] has made five [coins].' He said to him, 'And you, rule over five cities.' Then the other came, saying, 'Lord, here is your [coin]. I wrapped it up in a piece of cloth, for I was afraid of you, because you are a harsh man; you take what you did not deposit, and reap what you did not sow.' He said to him, 'I will judge you by your own words, you wicked slave! You knew, did you, that I was a harsh man, taking what I did not deposit and reaping what I did not sow? Why then did you not put my money into the bank? Then when I returned, I could have collected it with interest.' He said to the bystanders, 'Take the [coin] from him and give it to the one who has ten [coins].' (And they said to him, 'Lord, he has ten [coins]!') 'I tell you, to all those who have, more will be given; but from those who have nothing, even what they have will be taken away.' "

—Luke 19:12–26 NRSV

LET'S THINK

Some versions use the word "talents" for coins.
And the man gives his servants "gifts" to use for Him.
What talents has God given you?
How can you multiply your talents?

LET'S DO

Talk about how you can use your gifts for God.

LET'S PRAY

Thank You, God, for creating us with different talents and gifts.
Help us use them best to serve You. In Jesus' name, amen.

26

CHEERFUL GIVING

Remember this: The person who plants a little will have a small harvest. But the person who plants a lot will have a big harvest. Each one should give, then, what he has decided in his heart to give. He should not give if it makes him sad. And he should not give if he thinks he is forced to give. God loves the person who gives happily. And God can give you more blessings than you need. Then you will always have plenty of everything. You will have enough to give to every good work. It is written in the Scriptures: "He gives freely to the poor. The things he does are right and will continue forever."

—II Corinthians 9:6–9 ICB

Yes, God will give you much so that you can give away much, and when we take your gifts to those who need them they will break out into thanksgiving and praise to God for your help. So two good things happen as a result of your gifts—those in need are helped, and they overflow with thanks to God. Those you help will be glad not only because of your generous gifts to themselves and to others, but they will praise God for this proof that your deeds are as good as your doctrine. And they will pray for you with deep fervor and feeling because of the wonderful grace of God shown through you.

—II Corinthians 9:11–14 TLB

For most people, it's hard to share.
We are often concerned that we won't have enough for ourselves.
According to this scripture, that's not how God works.
What actually happens to our supply when we give?

...

Other than being able to give more,
what two good things happen when we give?

LET'S DO

Plan a way for your family to bless someone in your community or church family. Remember, God loves a cheerful giver!

LET'S PRAY

Thank You, God, for supplying all our needs. Help us be used by You by being cheerful givers. In Jesus' name, amen.

27

OPENING THE DOOR

When God's children are in need, you be the one to help them out. And get into the habit of inviting guests home for dinner or, if they need lodging, for the night.

—*Romans 12:13 TLB*

Cheerfully share your home with those who need a meal or a place to stay for the night.

—*1 Peter 4:9 TLB*

Dear friend, you are doing a good work for God in taking care of the traveling teachers and missionaries who are passing through. They have told the church here of your friendship and your loving deeds. I am glad when you send them on their way with a generous gift. For they are traveling for the Lord and take neither food, clothing, shelter, nor money from those who are not Christians, even though they have preached to them. So we ourselves should take care of them in order that we may become partners with them in the Lord's work.

—*III John 1:5–8 TLB*

Continue to love each other with true brotherly love. Don't forget to be kind to strangers, for some who have done this have entertained angels without realizing it!

—*Hebrews 13:1–2 TLB*

LET'S THINK

The Bible tells us that we are to be hospitable.
Who does the Bible tell us to help?
Hint: see if you can find at least five answers.
When helping them, who are you also helping?
Hint: Find at least two answers.
What kinds of things can we do to help others?
Hint: See if you can find seven or more answers.

...

In what ways were you treated with hospitality at someone's house?
What did they do to make you feel special?

LET'S DO

Plan to invite some friends over for a meal or play games.

...

Talk through some ways you can be hospitable
without inviting people into your home.
Hint: you can be kind to strangers anywhere.

LET'S PRAY

Thank You, God, for the ability to share what we have.
Help us show hospitality by being friendly and cheerfully
taking care of others' needs. In Jesus' name, amen.

TAKE TEN!

TAKE TURNS LETTING EACH FAMILY MEMBER ANSWER THE QUESTIONS BELOW.

About Others

1 Whose house do you like to visit and why?

2 Who makes you feel special and why?

3 What kind of family activities are your favorites?

About You

4 How do you like to serve others and why?

5 What are you naturally good at and how do you use those talents?

6 What has been your favorite age so far and why?

About Stuff

7 What are some of your favorite games?

8 What are some of your favorite stories or books?

9 What is one of your purposes in life?

10 In your family, how is each of you special?

28

WISDOM AND UNDERSTANDING

Get wisdom and understanding. Don't forget or ignore my words. Use wisdom, and it will take care of you. Love wisdom, and it will keep you safe. Wisdom is the most important thing. So get wisdom. If it costs everything you have, get understanding. Believe in the value of wisdom, and it will make you great. Use it, and it will bring honor to you.

—*Proverbs 4:5–8 ICB*

But if any of you needs wisdom, you should ask God for it. God is generous. He enjoys giving to all people, so God will give you wisdom.

—*James 1:5 ICB*

The Lord was pleased that Solomon had asked him for this [wisdom]. So God said to him, "You did not ask for a long life. And you did not ask for riches for yourself. You did not ask for the death of your enemies. Since you asked for wisdom to make the right decisions, I will give you what you asked. I will give you wisdom and understanding. Your wisdom will be greater than anyone has had in the past. And there will never be anyone in the future like you. Also, I will give you what you did not ask for. You will have riches and honor. During your life no other king will be as great as you."

—*I Kings 3:10–13 ICB*

LET'S THINK

Wisdom is more than knowing lots of stuff. Wisdom is using that knowledge and what you learn from experience to make good decisions based on what is true and right. Why is wisdom and understanding important?

•••

Think about some tough decisions when you really need wisdom.

•••

Think of a list of "wise sayings" like proverbs that your family uses often.

LET'S DO

Solomon wrote many wise sayings. These are from the book of Proverbs (ICB):

•••

When a wise person sees danger ahead, he avoids it.
But a foolish person keeps going and gets into trouble (22:3).

•••

Don't spend time with someone who has a bad temper.
If you do, you may learn to be like him (22:24–25).

•••

Remember what you are taught.
And listen carefully to words of knowledge (23:12).

LET'S PRAY

Dear God, please give us wisdom and understanding. Help us use it all the time, especially when we really need it. In Jesus' name, amen.

29

TRUTH AND HONESTY

The Lord hates those who tell lies. But He is pleased with those who do what they promise.

—*Proverbs 12:22 ICB*

A foolish person will believe anything. But a wise person thinks about what he does.

—*Proverbs 14:15 ICB*

A person shouldn't trick his neighbor and then say, "I was just joking!" That is like a madman shooting deadly, burning arrows.

—*Proverbs 26:18–19 ICB*

Lead good people down a wrong path and you'll come to a bad end; do good and you'll be rewarded for it.

—*Proverbs 28:10 THE MESSAGE*

LET'S THINK

Why are truth and honesty important?
Think about a difficult time when you were really glad you
told the truth. Why was it difficult to do so?

•••

It's also important to use wisdom to recognize when someone
else is telling the truth. What are ways to tell when someone is lying?
How can you "test" them without looking like a jerk?
Why is it good to hang out with honest people?

•••

Think about how tricking people can be dishonest and unkind.
Pulling pranks can be fun, but sometimes they can hurt people.
How do you know when it's okay to pull a prank?

LET'S DO

Have each family member share about a relationship
with someone who is honest and trustworthy.

LET'S PRAY

Dear God, please help us tell the truth even when it is difficult.
Help us be honest in a kind and loving way. Thank You for loving us.
In Jesus' name, amen.

30

A GUIDING LIGHT

Despise God's Word and find yourself in trouble. Obey it and succeed. The advice of a wise man refreshes like water from a mountain spring. Those accepting it become aware of the pitfalls on ahead.

—*Proverbs 13:13–14 TLB*

My child, listen to your father's teaching. And do not forget your mother's advice.

—*Proverbs 1:8 ICB*

[The priests] taught the true teachings. They spoke no lies. With peace and honesty they did what I [the Lord] said they should do. They kept many people from sinning.

—*Malachi 2:6 ICB*

All Scripture is inspired by God and is useful for teaching and for showing people what is wrong in their lives. It is useful for correcting faults and teaching how to live right.

—*II Timothy 3:16 ICB*

LET'S THINK

*Following instructions or the rules for a board game is easy.
It's all spelled out for you, usually on one page or in a small booklet.
Following God's instruction can be more difficult since the Bible is
thicker and has some complex concepts. Godly people like pastors,
teachers, grandparents, and parents can help make it easier to
understand. Why is it important to know what God instructs us
to do and do it?*

•••

*Why is it important to have godly people give us
instruction or advice?*

•••

*What ways can we make learning from the Bible
easier to understand and follow?*

LET'S DO

*Challenge each other to learn more about what God
instructs us to do. Talk about how you can make that happen.*

LET'S PRAY

*Dear God, please help us follow godly instruction. Help us know what
You want us to do. Thank You for loving us. In Jesus' name, amen.*

31

SHOUTS OF JOY

I celebrate and shout because you are kind. You saw all my suffering, and You cared for me.

—*Psalm 31:7 CEV*

I will always praise the LORD. With all my heart, I will praise the LORD. Let all who are helpless, listen and be glad. Honor the LORD with me! Celebrate His great name. I asked the LORD for help, and He saved me from all my fears. . . . I was a nobody, but I prayed, and the LORD saved me from all my troubles.

—*Psalm 34:1–4, 6 CEV*

My brothers, you will have many kinds of troubles. But when these things happen, you should be very happy. You know that these things are testing your faith. And this will give you patience. Let your patience show itself perfectly in what you do. Then you will be perfect and complete. You will have everything you need.

—*James 1:2–4 ICB*

Do everything without grumbling or arguing.

—*Philippians 2:14 CEV*

It's easy to get caught up in grumbling and complaining.
Everyone does it—kids too. Parents usually call it whining.
What are some recent complaints you've heard?
Do you think God cares about all of them? Why?

•••

Troubles come from anywhere. These troubles test us.
When we fail, God forgives us. When we succeed, we learn patience.
How can we be joyful when bad things happen?

LET'S DO

Doing things we don't want to do without complaining is nearly
impossible! This challenge is going to require God's help. The next time
you are frustrated, try not to complain about it. Ask God to help you.
If you fail, ask for forgiveness and try again!

•••

Talk about things you are grateful for and how God shows you He cares.

LET'S PRAY

Dear God, please give us a joyful heart even when things don't
go our way. Help us see that You care about us no matter what.
In Jesus' name, amen.

32

SPEAK NO EVIL

A person who gossips can't keep secrets. But a trustworthy person can keep a secret.

—Proverbs 11:13 ICB

Whoever forgives someone's sin makes a friend. But the one who tells about the sin breaks up friendships.

—Proverbs 17:9 ICB

When you talk, do not say harmful things. But say what people need—words that will help others become stronger. Then what you say will help those who listen to you.

—Ephesians 4:29 ICB

Remind the believers to do these things: to be under the authority of rulers and government leaders, to obey them and be ready to do good, to speak no evil about anyone, to live in peace with all, to be gentle and polite to all people.

—Titus 3:1–2 ICB

Lord, help me control my tongue. Help me be careful about what I say.

—Psalm 141:3 ICB

LET'S THINK

No one likes a gossip. Someone who gossips tells others things that are none of their business and may not be true. What can be categorized as gossip? How do you feel when others talk about you behind your back?

•••

Trustworthy people make good friends.
What makes a friend trustworthy?

•••

You may have heard the saying, "T.H.I.N.K. before you speak." Is it True? Helpful? Inspiring? Necessary? Kind? These are really good questions to ask ourselves before we start blabbing.

LET'S DO

We cannot control what others think or say about us or others. But we can control our own tongue with God's help. If others are saying mean things about a friend, you can stick up for them and put an end to it. Talk with each other about how.

•••

Practice speaking encouraging words. What can you say to another that will help them become stronger?

LET'S PRAY

Dear God, please help me control my tongue. Help me be careful about what I say. Thank You that You love us, that we can trust You, and that You will be our best friend forever. In Jesus' name, amen.

ENCOURAGING WORDS

A person without good sense finds fault with his neighbor. But a person with understanding keeps quiet.

—*Proverbs 11:12 ICB*

People enjoy giving good answers! Saying the right word at the right time is so pleasing!

—*Proverbs 15:23 ICB*

Encourage anyone who feels left out, help all who are weak, and be patient with everyone.

—*I Thessalonians 5:14 CEV*

God has also given each of us different gifts to use. . . . If we can encourage others, we should encourage them.

—*Romans 12:6, 8 CEV*

Lord, help me control my tongue. Help me be careful about what I say.

—*Psalm 141:3 ICB*

LET'S THINK

En- in front of the word courage means to "help become courageous." Words with a similar meaning to encourage are motivate, urge, coax, and support. Think of different ways your family has encouraged you.

•••

Dis- in front of courage means the opposite. Words that have a similar meaning to discourage are dishearten, demoralize, and put a stop to, as well as the idea of name-calling. God doesn't like it when people make fun of each other. Have you ever felt discouraged or left out? Have you noticed someone else who felt that way? How can you encourage them?

LET'S DO

The next time you see someone discouraged, give them an encouraging word! Try to inspire them to succeed.

•••

Just for fun! Role-play some situations and think about how you should handle them. Start with this: It is Victor and Violet's first day. They don't know where to get lunch. What do you do?

LET'S PRAY

Dear God, please help me be an encourager. Help me when I am discouraged. Thank You that You love us. Thank You for giving us family and friends who encourage us. In Jesus' name, amen.

34

WISDOM IN ANGER

People who make fun of others cause trouble in a city. But wise people calm anger down.

—Proverbs 29:8 ICB

It's smart to be patient, but it's stupid to lose your temper.

—Proverbs 14:29 CEV

Don't repay evil for evil. Wait for the Lord to handle the matter.

—Proverbs 20:22 TLB

See to it that no one repays evil for evil to anyone, but always pursue what is good for one another and for all.

—I Thessalonians 5:15 CSB

Do you know where your fights and arguments come from? They come from the selfish desires that make war inside you. You want things, but you do not have them. So you are ready to kill and are jealous of other people. But you still cannot get what you want. So you argue and fight. You do not get what you want because you do not ask God.

—James 4:1–2 ICB

LET'S THINK

It's easy to get angry when things don't go our way or when others say mean things about us or do unkind things. We can make others angry when we do these things to them. The Bible is full of good advice on handling these situations.

...

Think about what makes you angry. What shouldn't we do when we are angry? What should we do when we are angry? How you could handle a situation better next time?

...

What does James tell us we are fighting with before we actually fight and argue with people? What can we do about that?

LET'S DO

Take a moment to pray silently for those who have been mean to you. Ask God for the best way to respond.

LET'S PRAY

Dear God, help us get our hearts in the right place. Help us care about everyone the way You do. In Jesus' name, amen.

35

LAZY SLOTHS

The lazy person may put his hand in the dish. But he's too tired to lift the food to his mouth.

—*Proverbs 26:15 ICB*

Those who work hard make a profit. But those who only talk will be poor.

—*Proverbs 14:23 ICB*

People who refuse to work are not following the teaching that we gave them. You yourselves know that you should live as we live. We were not lazy when we were with you. And when we ate another person's food, we always paid for it. We worked and worked so that we would not be a trouble to any of you. We worked night and day. We had the right to ask you to help us. But we worked to take care of ourselves so that we would be an example for you to follow. When we were with you, we gave you this rule: "If anyone will not work, he will not eat."

We hear that some people in your group refuse to work. They do nothing. And they busy themselves in other people's lives. We command those people to work quietly and earn their own food. In the Lord Jesus Christ we beg them to do this.

—*II Thessalonians 3:6–12 ICB*

LET'S THINK

Sloths really aren't lazy. Sloths are just so slow that they look lazy. People who move like sloths when a job needs to get done are lazy! Picture the first verse. Now that's a lazy person! What do the other proverbs tell us about lazy people? What do they tell us about hard workers?

•••

Paul's letter warns the Thessalonians about being lazy. What good examples does he give about working? What were the lazy people doing instead of working?

LET'S DO

The next time someone asks you to do a job for them, don't drag it out. Work quickly and efficiently. And Paul says, "Work quietly." What do you suppose that means? Can you do that too?

LET'S PRAY

Dear God, help us work quickly and efficiently without complaining. Thank You for giving us good examples like Paul and his friends. Help us learn from them and be hard workers. In Jesus' name, amen.

36

LOVE IS NOT JEALOUS

I [Solomon] realized the reason people work hard and try to succeed: They are jealous of each other. This, too, is useless . . . I say it is better to be content with what little you have. Otherwise, you will always be struggling for more. That is like chasing the wind.

—*Ecclesiastes 4:4–6 ICB*

In the past we were foolish people, too. We did not obey, we were wrong, and we were slaves to many things our bodies wanted and enjoyed . . . But then the kindness and love of God our Savior was shown.

—*Titus 3:3–4 ICB*

Whenever people are jealous or selfish, they cause trouble and do all sorts of cruel things. But the wisdom that comes from above leads us to be pure, friendly, gentle, sensible, kind, helpful, genuine, and sincere.

—*James 3:16–17 CEV*

Love is patient and kind. Love is not jealous. . . .

—*I Corinthians 13:4 ICB*

LET'S THINK

It sure is nice to be content. The world would be a much better place if we all were. We'd all be satisfied and happy. "World peace" would actually be a possibility. How does jealousy and envy cause people to hate and not get along?

...

Don't be discouraged! The kindness and love of Jesus is here. The wisdom of God will help us be different. How should we behave if we have God's love and wisdom? Hint: the verse in James has a list!

LET'S DO

Invite each family member to talk about a time they wanted something someone else had and how it made them feel.

...

Talk about things you have to be thankful for.

LET'S PRAY

Dear God, help us be content. Thank You for giving us wonderful things like _____. Help us be grateful and at peace. In Jesus' name, amen.

TAKE TEN!

TAKE TURNS LETTiNG EACH FAMiLY MEMBER ANSWER THE QUESTiONS BELOW.

About Others

1 Who gives you good advice and why?

2 Who makes you angry and why?

3 What makes someone a good worker?

About You

4 When is it hard to tell the truth?

5 What kind of compliments do you like to get?

6   What jobs do you like to work hard at?

About Stuff

7   What are some things you wish you had?

8   Where are some places you'd like to go?

9   What is more important to you than the answers for #7 and 8?

10   How can you show that you are grateful?

37

LOVE EACH OTHER

Your love must be real. Hate what is evil. Hold on to what is good. Love each other like brothers and sisters. Give your brothers and sisters more honor than you want for yourselves. . . . Wish good for those who do bad things to you. Wish them well and do not curse them. . . . Live together in peace with each other. Do not be proud, but make friends with those who seem unimportant. Do not think how smart you are. If someone does wrong to you, do not pay him back by doing wrong to him. Try to do what everyone thinks is right. Do your best to live in peace with everyone. My friends, do not try to punish others when they wrong you. Wait for God to punish them with His anger. It is written: "I am the One who punishes; I will pay people back," says the Lord. But you should do this: "If your enemy is hungry, feed him; if your enemy is thirsty, give him a drink. Doing this will be like pouring burning coals on his head." Do not let evil defeat you. Defeat evil by doing good.

—*Romans 12:9–10, 14, 16–21 ICB*

LET'S THINK

This part of Paul's letter written to the Romans has a lot of challenges—especially if you're dealing with bullies! How can you respond in the right way when you are bullied?

•••

There are challenges even if you simply want to be a good friend. Which three do you find the most difficult to do? Why?

LET'S DO

Paul tells us to love others like we love our brothers and sisters. Sometimes brothers and sisters are the most difficult people to love—because they know how to drive us nuts! Let's flip it around and consider how to be lovable. Talk about what we could (and should) do to make it easier for our brothers, sisters, and family to love us.

•••

Challenge yourself this week to honor your family and treat them better than you would want to be treated.

LET'S PRAY

Dear God, help us behave in loving ways and in treating others better than we want to be treated. Please help us stick up for those who are being treated badly. In Jesus' name, amen.

HELP IS ON THE WAY!

I love the Lord because He listens to my prayers for help. He paid attention to me. So I will call to Him for help as long as I live. The ropes of death bound me. The fear of death took hold of me. I was troubled and sad. Then I called out the name of the Lord. I said, "Please, Lord, save me!" . . . I said to myself, "Relax, because the Lord takes care of you."

—*Psalm 116:1–4, 7 ICB*

Lord, remember my suffering and how I have no home. Remember the misery and suffering. I remember them well. And I am very sad. But I have hope when I think of this: The Lord's love never ends. His mercies never stop. They are new every morning. Lord, Your loyalty is great. I say to myself, "The Lord is what I have left. So I have hope." The Lord is good to those who put their hope in Him. He is good to those who look to Him for help. It is good to wait quietly for the Lord to save.

—*Lamentations 3:19–26 ICB*

LET'S THINK

What do you do when you feel helpless and afraid? We read that the psalmist was sad and even "scared to death." It was then that he called out to God for help. What happened when he prayed?

•••

The prophet Jeremiah probably wrote the passage in Lamentations. A lament is a fancy way of saying "crying your eyes out." Jeremiah was suffering and so miserable that he cried his eyes out to the Lord. Have you ever been that upset?

•••

Jeremiah finds hope in the Lord. What does Jeremiah think of when he needs hope? Are you waiting with hope for something? What is it?

LET'S DO

Talk about situations where someone may feel hopeless. Put yourself in their shoes and role-play a prayer about asking God for help.

•••

Challenge: If you feel comfortable, talk about a time when you felt hopeless. Take time to pray together and tell God about the details.

LET'S PRAY

Dear God, help us relax and know that You are in charge. Don't let us forget to call on You to help us when we are overwhelmed. Thank You for giving us hope. In Jesus' name, amen.

39

HELP IS HERE!

My help comes from the Lord. He made heaven and earth.

—*Psalm 121:2 ICB*

Praise God, the Father of our Lord Jesus Christ! The Father is a merciful God, who always gives us comfort. He comforts us when we are in trouble, so that we can share that same comfort with others in trouble. We share in the terrible sufferings of Christ, but also in the wonderful comfort He gives. We suffer in the hope that you will be comforted and saved. And because we are comforted, you will also be comforted, as you patiently endure suffering like ours. You never disappoint us. You suffered as much as we did, and we know that you will be comforted as we were.

My friends, I want you to know what a hard time we had in Asia. Our sufferings were so horrible and so unbearable that death seemed certain. In fact, we felt sure that we were going to die. But this made us stop trusting in ourselves and start trusting God, who raises the dead to life. God saved us from the threat of death, and we are sure that He will do it again and again.

Please help us by praying for us. Then many people will give thanks for the blessings we receive in answer to all these prayers.

—*II Corinthians 1:3–11 CEV*

LET'S THINK

Paul and Timothy suffered a lot when they traveled throughout Asia, telling people about Christ's saving love. Sometimes we feel like no one could ever know how we feel. No one could understand. Paul suffered so much that he nearly died several times. And here he is, encouraging us!

•••

How does Paul encourage us in these passages?
What good thing comes from suffering?
How does Paul ask for help? What does God provide?

LET'S DO

Talk about some Bible stories where God helped His people. One crazy, exciting story you'll want to read is when Peter was rescued from prison by angels in Acts 12:1–18.

•••

Be an encouragement to others.
Find someone to pray with or for this week.

LET'S PRAY

Dear God, we know You will comfort us and come to our rescue. You saved Paul and Timothy from death and Peter from prison. Thanks for helping us too! In Jesus' name, amen.

40

TEN LEPERS

Jesus was on his way to Jerusalem. Traveling from Galilee to Samaria, He came into a small town. Ten men met Him there. These men did not come close to Jesus, because they all had a harmful skin disease. But they called to Him, "Jesus! Master! Please help us!"

—*Luke 17:11–13 ICB*

Jesus looked at them and said, "Go show yourselves to the priests." On their way they were healed. When one of them discovered that he was healed, he came back, shouting praises to God. He bowed down at the feet of Jesus and thanked Him. The man was from the country of Samaria. Jesus asked, "Weren't ten men healed? Where are the other nine? Why was this foreigner the only one who came back to thank God?" Then Jesus told the man, "You may get up and go. Your faith has made you well."

—*Luke 17:14–19 CEV*

Always be happy. Never stop praying. Give thanks whatever happens. That is what God wants for you in Christ Jesus.

—*I Thessalonians 5:16–18 ICB*

LET'S THINK

Some things we ask Jesus for might seem silly. Maybe we don't think Jesus finds our request important enough to bother asking Him. But we are important to Jesus, so ask! What have you asked Jesus to do?

•••

Jesus thinks it's important for us to thank Him for answering prayers. How did the leper thank Jesus?

•••

Sometimes we take for granted all the wonderful things God does for us. Why do you think the other lepers didn't come back to thank Jesus? Why don't we remember to thank Jesus?

LET'S DO

Roll call! Time for every family member to name three things they are thankful to God for.

•••

Paul tells us to be thankful no matter what happens. That means that even when God doesn't answer our prayers like we think He should, we should be joyful!

LET'S PRAY

Dear God, help us appreciate everything You have done. Thank You for helping us with so many things, even if they seem small and silly to others. Thanks for loving us. In Jesus' name, amen.

THANKS FOR OTHER FOLKS

Give my greetings to Priscilla and Aquila, who work together with me in Christ Jesus. They risked their own lives to save my life. I am thankful to them.

—*Romans 16:3–4 ICB*

I am very happy in the Lord that you have shown your care for me again ... It was good that you helped me when I needed help.

—*Philippians 4:10, 14 ICB*

We have so much joy before our God because of you, and we thank Him for you. But we cannot thank Him enough for all the joy we feel. And we continue praying with all our heart for you night and day. We pray that we can see you again and give you all the things you need to make your faith strong.

—*I Thessalonians 3:9–10 ICB*

Philemon, each time I mention you in my prayers, I thank God. I hear about your faith in our Lord Jesus and about your love for all of God's people . . . My friend, your love has made me happy and has greatly encouraged me. It has also cheered the hearts of God's people.

—*Philemon 1:4–7 CEV*

LET'S THINK

God is who we owe the most thanks to—but we should also thank people. And ultimately we thank God for those people! Paul sets a good example when he writes to the churches in Rome, Philippi, and Thessalonica. Who do you appreciate and thank God for?

...

Philemon was a personal friend of Paul's who loved Jesus and God's people. Paul personally writes to Philemon and the church meeting in his home. How can we show others that they are special to God and to us?

LET'S DO

Take time this week to thank someone who helps or inspires you. Even a quick text, phone call, or thank-you note will do.

LET'S PRAY

Dear God, help us appreciate our friends. Thanks for giving us people to encourage and help us. Thanks for loving us. In Jesus' name, amen.

42

THANKSGIVING

Come, let's sing for joy to the Lord. Let's shout praises to the Rock who saves us. Let's come to Him with thanksgiving. Let's sing songs to Him. The Lord is the great God. He is the great King over all gods. The deepest places on earth are His. And the highest mountains belong to Him. The sea is His because He made it. He created the land with His own hands. Come, let's bow down and worship Him. Let's kneel before the Lord who made us. He is our God. And we are the people He takes care of and the sheep that He tends.

—*Psalm 95:1–7 ICB*

Thank GOD because He's good, because His love never quits. Tell the world, Israel, "His love never quits." And you, clan of Aaron, tell the world, "His love never quits." And you who fear GOD, join in, "His love never quits."

—*Psalm 118:1–4 THE MESSAGE*

Give thanks in all circumstances; for this is the will of God in Christ Jesus for you.

—*I Thessalonians 5:18 ESV*

Always be thankful.

—*Colossians 3:15 ICB*

Today is probably not Thanksgiving Day. But that certainly doesn't mean that we can't be grateful for what God has done for us! The Psalm 95 passage brings us back to the beginning, praising God for making the world and everything in it. What other things can you find to thank God for? What different ways can we show our appreciation to God when we thank Him?

•••

Psalm 118 thanks God for being good and His never-quitting love. Why do you think God's people need to repeat it so many times?

•••

When should we be thankful?

LET'S DO

Thank God in a different way this week. Maybe sing a song. Maybe change your posture and kneel. What about dancing, jumping, or shouting for joy?

LET'S PRAY

Dear God, help us be thankful all the time. Thank You for creating the world for us to enjoy. Thanks for Your never-ending love for us. In Jesus' name, amen.

43

GOT FAITH? WALKING ON WATER

Between three and six o'clock in the morning, Jesus' followers were still in the boat. Jesus came to them. He was walking on the water. When the followers saw Him walking on the water, they were afraid. They said, "It's a ghost!" and cried out in fear.

. . . He said, "Have courage! It is I! Don't be afraid."

Peter said, "Lord, if that is really You, then tell me to come to You on the water."

Jesus said, "Come."

And Peter left the boat and walked on the water to Jesus. But when Peter saw the wind and the waves, he became afraid and began to sink. He shouted, "Lord, save me!"

Then Jesus reached out His hand and caught Peter. Jesus said, "Your faith is small. Why did you doubt?"

After Peter and Jesus were in the boat, the wind became calm. Then those who were in the boat worshiped Jesus and said, "Truly You are the Son of God!"

—*Matthew 14:25–33 ICB*

"Remember that I commanded you to be strong and brave . . . The Lord your God will be with you everywhere you go."

—*Joshua 1:9 ICB*

I can do all things through Christ because He gives me strength.

—*Philippians 4:13 ICB*

LET'S THINK

Peter might have been afraid like his friends—but he responded differently. Whether it was craziness or courage, he challenged Jesus. Surprisingly, Jesus took the opportunity to prove that He was God. What do you think was going through the minds of the others—and Peter, when he took that first step out of the boat? Why did Peter sink?

•••

Sometimes we fail, even if we think we have enough courage and strength before we start. What did Peter do when he began to sink? How did Jesus respond?

LET'S DO

Don't be afraid to take the first step. God's got it! What will you do with His help?

LET'S PRAY

Dear God, help us be strong and courageous. Help us take the first step. Be with us along the way. Thanks for loving us. In Jesus' name, amen.

44

GOT FAITH? JESUS HEALS THE CRIPPLED MAN

Jesus went back to Capernaum, and a few days later people heard that He was at home. Then so many of them came to the house that there wasn't even standing room left in front of the door.

Jesus was still teaching when four people came up, carrying a crippled man on a mat. But because of the crowd, they could not get him to Jesus. So they made a hole in the roof above Him and let the man down in front of everyone.

When Jesus saw how much faith they had, He said to the crippled man, "My friend, your sins are forgiven."

Some of the teachers of the Law of Moses were sitting there. They started wondering, "Why would He say such a thing? He must think He is God! Only God can forgive sins."

Right away, Jesus knew what they were thinking, and He said, "Why are you thinking such things? Is it easier for Me to tell this crippled man that his sins are forgiven or to tell him to get up and pick up his mat and go on home? I will show you that the Son of Man has the right to forgive sins here on earth." So Jesus said to the man, "Get up! Pick up your mat and go on home."

The man got right up. He picked up his mat and went out while everyone watched in amazement. They praised God and said, "We have never seen anything like this!"

—Mark 2:1–12 CEV

LET'S THINK

The man's friends were determined to get him to Jesus. They had to think of a way around their problem. Their faith proved that their efforts were worth it.

•••

Think about someone who took a step of faith and saw God follow through. How did God show His power?

•••

There's another miracle in this passage too—Jesus forgave the man's sin. That's not possible to see. Believing that God forgives and cares . . . well, that also takes a step of faith. How can we know that God loves and forgives us?

LET'S DO

Pray expecting God to come through.

LET'S PRAY

Dear God, thank You for all your miraculous ways. Open my eyes to see Your love and power every day of my life. In Jesus' name, amen.

45

GOT FAITH? LAZARUS LIVES

Martha said to Jesus, "Lord, if You had been here, my brother would not have died. Yet even now I know that God will do anything You ask."

. . . Jesus then said, "I am the One who raises the dead to life! Everyone who has faith in Me will live, even if they die. And everyone who lives because of faith in Me will never really die. Do you believe this?"

"Yes, Lord!" she replied. "I believe that you are Christ, the Son of God. . . ."

Mary went to where Jesus was. Then as soon as she saw Him, she knelt at His feet and said, "Lord, if You had been here, my brother would not have died."

. . . Jesus was still terribly upset. So He went to the tomb, which was a cave with a stone rolled against the entrance. Then He told the people to roll the stone away. But Martha said, "Lord, You know that Lazarus has been dead four days, and there will be a bad smell."

Jesus replied, "Didn't I tell you that if you had faith, you would see the glory of God?"

After the stone had been rolled aside, Jesus looked up toward heaven and prayed, "Father, I thank you for answering My prayer. I know that You always answer My prayers. But I said this, so that the people here would believe that You sent Me."

When Jesus had finished praying, He shouted, "Lazarus, come out!" The man who had been dead came out. . . .

—John 11:14–15, 21–27, 32, 35–44 CEV

LET'S THINK

Lazarus's sisters, Mary and Martha, thought that Jesus had failed them. What did He want them to learn?

LET'S DO

Make a list of things to pray for. Title it "God's got this!" and then know, without a doubt, that God is bigger than any worry or concern you may have.

LET'S PRAY

Dear God, strengthen our faith. Help us trust that, in the end, You've still got it. In Jesus' name, amen.

TAKE TEN!

TAKE TURNS LETTING EACH FAMILY MEMBER ANSWER THE QUESTIONS BELOW.

About Others

1. What makes someone a good friend?

2. What might others appreciate about you?

3. What modern-day miracles have you experienced?

About You

4. What do you look for in a friend?

5. What do you like about Thanksgiving?

6   Which miraculous event from the Bible
    would you have liked to witness?

About Stuff

7   What are you thankful for?

8   What are fun things you like to do
    with friends?

9   What is something a friend needs help with
    that you (and your family) could do?

10 Who do you know with a strong faith,
    and how do you know that?

LITTLE THINGS, HUGE IMPACTS

One day the widow of one of the LORD's prophets said to Elisha, "You know that before my husband died, he was a follower of yours and a worshiper of the LORD. But he owed a man some money, and now that man is on his way to take my two sons as his slaves."

"Maybe there's something I can do to help," Elisha said. "What do you have in your house?"

"Sir, I have nothing but a small bottle of olive oil."

Elisha told her, "Ask your neighbors for their empty jars. And after you've borrowed as many as you can, go home and shut the door behind you and your sons. Then begin filling the jars with oil and set each one aside as you fill it." The woman left.

Later, when she and her sons were back inside their house, the two sons brought her the jars, and she began filling them.

At last, she said to one of her sons, "Bring me another jar."

"We don't have any more," he answered, and the oil stopped flowing from the small bottle.

After she told Elisha what had happened, he said, "Sell the oil and use part of the money to pay what you owe the man. You and your sons can live on what is left."

—II Kings 4:1–7 CEV

LET'S THINK

God was able to work through Elisha to help a poor widow. This miracle would have been really cool to see! If you are a grown-up, imagine that you are the widow. Kids, imagine that you are about to be taken away to be slaves. How do you feel, knowing your family has nothing left but a little jar of oil? What are you thinking when Elisha tells you to borrow jars from your neighbors?

LET'S DO

With God's help, Elisha helped the widow by using the one little thing she had. Is there a little thing you can use to help someone this week?

LET'S PRAY

Dear God, thanks for helping us when we need it. Thanks for people who help us when we have nothing left to give. In Jesus' name, amen.

47

BE A GIVER, NOT A TAKER

While all the people were listening, Jesus said to His followers, "Be careful of the teachers of the law. They like to walk around wearing clothes that look important. And they love for people to show respect to them in the marketplaces. They love to have the most important seats in the synagogues and at the feasts. But they cheat widows and steal their houses. Then they try to make themselves look good by saying long prayers. God will punish these men very much."

—Luke 20:45–47 ICB

Jesus saw some rich people putting their gifts into the Temple money box. Then Jesus saw a poor widow. She put two small copper coins into the box. He said, "I tell you the truth. This poor widow gave only two small coins. But she really gave more than all those rich people. The rich have plenty; they gave only what they did not need. This woman is very poor, but she gave all she had. And she needed that money to live on."

—Luke 21:1–4 ICB

Don't be jealous or proud, but be humble and consider others more important than yourselves. Care about them as much as you care about yourselves.

—Philippians 2:3–4 CEV

LET'S THINK

Right in front of those wealthy visitors, a poor widow gave all she had to the temple—only a couple of cents! What did Jesus think of that?

•••

Think about what Jesus accused the rich guys of doing to widows. Even after potentially being cheated and stolen from or losing her house, this widow gave all she had left to the Lord's temple. What did Jesus think?

LET'S DO

Talk about what you have to give.
How can you care for someone this week?

LET'S PRAY

Dear God, help us look past ourselves to see people in need. Show me what I can do to give. Thanks for loving us. In Jesus' name, amen.

GOD MULTIPLIES GENEROSITY

Remember this: The person who plants a little will have a small harvest. But the person who plants a lot will have a big harvest. Each one should give, then, what he has decided in his heart to give. He should not give if it makes him sad. And he should not give if he thinks he is forced to give. God loves the person who gives happily. And God can give you more blessings than you need. Then you will always have plenty of everything. You will have enough to give to every good work . . . "He gives freely to the poor. The things He does are right and will continue forever." God is the One who gives seed to the farmer. And He gives bread for food . . . God will make you rich in every way so that you can always give freely.

—II Corinthians 9:6–11 ICB

If you give to others, you will be given a full amount in return. It will be packed down, shaken together, and spilling over into your lap.

—Luke 6:38 CEV

When you do good deeds, don't try to show off. If you do, you won't get a reward from your Father in heaven. . . . When you give to the poor, don't let anyone know about it . . . Your Father knows what is done in secret, and He will reward you.

—Matthew 6:1, 3–4 CEV

LET'S THINK

What do you think of these Scriptures? Life isn't all about getting. But getting is part of it. What we have, we get from God; then we give to others and He gives us more!

•••

What are some stipulations for giving? If you follow these "rules," what will you (eventually) get in return?

•••

Think about the farmer. Come up with ways in which God multiplies generosity.

LET'S DO

Talk about what you have to give. If you need ideas, read Mark 12:41–44. Then make plans to do it!

LET'S PRAY

Dear God, thanks for everything You have given us. Help us be cheerful givers. Thanks for loving us. In Jesus' name, amen.

49

ASK GOD

[After he arrived, Abraham's] servant said, "Lord, you are the God of my master Abraham. Allow me to find a wife for his son today. Please show this kindness to my master Abraham. Here I am, standing by the spring of water. The girls from the city are coming out to get water. I will say to one of the girls, 'Please put your jar down so I can drink.' Then let her say, 'Drink, and I will also give water to your camels.' If that happens, I will know she is the right one for your servant Isaac. And I will know that you have shown kindness to my master."

Before the servant had finished praying, Rebekah came out of the city. . . . She was very pretty. . . .

She went down to the spring and filled her jar. Then she came back up. The servant ran to her and said, "Please give me a little water from your jar."

Rebekah said, "Drink, sir." She quickly lowered the jar from her shoulder and gave him a drink. After he finished drinking, Rebekah said, "I will also pour some water for your camels." So she quickly poured all the water from her jar into the drinking trough for the camels. Then she kept running to the well until she had given all the camels enough to drink.

—Genesis 24:12–20 ICB

LET'S THINK

There is a lot of asking going on in this part of the story! Abraham asked his servant to find a wife for his son, Isaac. The servant prayed to God and asked for guidance in order to find the right woman. And then the servant asked a pretty girl for a drink of water. How many requests were answered? What can you learn from each one of them?

...

Rebekah went "above and beyond" when doing what the servant asked. What personality traits did this show the servant? What kind of characteristics would Abraham want his daughter-in-law to have?

LET'S DO

Roll call! Time for each family member to talk through a tough decision they had to make. Tell how God helped in each situation. Remember, the next time you have a tough decision in front of you and you don't have a clue about what to do, ask God!

LET'S PRAY

Dear God, thanks for loving us and for answering our prayers. Give us wisdom about how to ask for help and recognize the right and wrong answers. In Jesus' name, amen.

50

ASK AND IT WILL BE GIVEN

Ask, and you will receive. . . . As bad as you are, you still know how to give good gifts to your children. But your heavenly Father is even more ready to give good things to people who ask.

—*Matthew 7:7, 11 CEV*

The Father will give you whatever you ask for in My name. You have not asked for anything in this way before, but now you must ask in My name. Then it will be given to you, so that you will be completely happy. . . . You will ask the Father in My name, and I won't have to ask Him for you. God the Father loves you because you love Me, and you believe that I have come from Him.

—*John 16:23–24, 26–27 CEV*

We are certain that God will hear our prayers when we ask for what pleases Him. And if we know that God listens when we pray, we are sure that our prayers have already been answered.

—*1 John 5:14–15 CEV*

LET'S THINK

People have different ideas about asking God for stuff. Some say, "He's too busy" or "It's not important." But others say, "Go ahead, ask!" What do you think? What does the Bible tell us?

...

We are to ask God in faith, without doubting. And what else? Hint: In Jesus' _____.

...

Sometimes we don't get the answers we want—or we don't hear an answer at all. What does the Bible tell us about that? What kinds of things does Jesus say His Father will give us if we ask?

LET'S DO

Now you know why we say "In Jesus' name." What about "amen"? Amen means "so be it." It comes from the Hebrew word "āmēn" which means certainly or truly. By saying it together, we agree with each other and God. Ask in Jesus' name and say amen!

LET'S PRAY

Dear God, thanks for loving us, hearing us, and answering our prayers. Help us ask for good things. In Jesus' name, amen.

51

SAY AGAIN

Then Jesus used this story to teach His followers that they should always pray and never lose hope. "Once there was a judge in a town. He did not care about God. He also did not care what people thought about him. In that same town there was a widow who kept coming to this judge. She said, 'There is a man who is not being fair to me. Give me my rights!' But the judge did not want to help the widow. After a long time, he thought to himself, 'I don't care about God. And I don't care about what people think. But this widow is bothering me. I will see that she gets her rights, or she will bother me until I am worn out!'"

The Lord said, "Listen to what the bad judge said. God's people cry to him night and day. God will always give them what is right, and He will not be slow to answer them. I tell you, God will help His people quickly! But when the Son of Man comes again, will He find those on earth who believe in Him?"

—Luke 18:1–8 ICB

LET'S THINK

When things are crumbling around us and everything looks bleak, we ask for help—but when help never comes, we can lose hope. The Bible tells us not to give up!

•••

Who does Jesus compare the widow and the judge to? What are the similarities and differences between the comparison? Why is God better than any earthly judge?

•••

Jesus ends His story with what could be considered an out-of-place question. Why do you suppose He asks, "Will I find anyone who believes in Me when I come back to earth?"

LET'S DO

When we are frustrated and lose hope, remember this story! Be encouraged by what Jesus tells us. Ask again; don't give up. The judge didn't care about the widow and her problems. God on the other hand, loves us so much and even cares about little things. He actually knows the number of hairs on our head! (See Matthew 10:30.)

LET'S PRAY

Dear God, thanks for loving us and answering our prayers. Give us hope and the faith that You will come through for us. Help us believe this is true. In Jesus' name, amen.

GIFTED AND TALENTED

Every good action and every perfect gift is from God.

—*James 1:17 ICB*

But each person has his own gift from God. One has one gift, another has another gift.

—*1 Corinthians 7:7 ICB*

The Lord has given them the skill to do all kinds of work. They are able to cut designs in metal and stone. They can plan and sew designs in the fine linen with the blue, purple and red thread. And they are also able to weave things.

—*Exodus 35:35 ICB*

God has also given each of us different gifts to use. If we can prophesy, we should do it according to the amount of faith we have. If we can serve others, we should serve. If we can teach, we should teach. If we can encourage others, we should encourage them. If we can give, we should be generous. If we are leaders, we should do our best. If we are good to others, we should do it cheerfully.

—*Romans 12:6–8 CEV*

LET'S THINK

Maybe you have heard something like: "She is so talented." "What a gift he has for drawing." "It's as if he were born to run!" Or, "Her singing is so beautiful." Maybe they are talking about you! Perhaps you had a great coach or fabulous teacher, or an amazing opportunity fell into your lap. Think about who made that happen.

•••

Where do talents come from? God has created each of us for a special purpose. Some people may feel as if they are not good at anything—but Paul tells the Romans that we each have different gifts! What did God gift you with?

LET'S DO

Talk about how to use and develop your gifts. Take a step to uncover or grow your talents. Plan to take a class or practice—knowing that God gave you your gifts to enjoy and use to bless others.

LET'S PRAY

Dear God, thanks for creating us with special abilities. Help us discover what we're made for. Show us how to use our gifts to bless others. In Jesus' name, amen.

53

EXCEPTIONAL GIFTS

Now, brothers, I want you to understand about spiritual gifts. . . There are different kinds of gifts; but they are all from the same Spirit. There are different ways to serve; but all these ways are from the same Lord. And there are different ways that God works in people; but all these ways are from the same God. God works in us all in everything we do. Something from the Spirit can be seen in each person, to help everyone. The Spirit gives one person the ability to speak with wisdom. And the same Spirit gives another the ability to speak with knowledge. The same Spirit gives faith to one person. And that one Spirit gives another gifts of healing. The Spirit gives to another person the power to do miracles, to another the ability to prophesy. And He gives to another the ability to know the difference between good and evil spirits. The Spirit gives one person the ability to speak in different kinds of languages and to another the ability to interpret those languages.

—I Corinthians 12:1, 4–10 ICB

Each of you received a spiritual gift. God has shown you His grace in giving you different gifts. And you are like servants who are responsible for using God's gifts. So be good servants and use your gifts to serve each other.

—I Peter 4:10 ICB

LET'S THINK

These gifts are extra special—Spiritual gifts. You could kind of think of them like superpowers that God gives, but not exactly. This is not an entire list, but they include preaching, helping, leading, and more.

•••

How are spiritual gifts similar to superpowers?
Why are they not at all like superpowers? Which gifts seem ordinary?
Which ones seem extraordinary?

LET'S DO

Talk about gifts you have. How do you use them to help others?

•••

Talk about special gifts you would like to have.
How would you use them to help others?

LET'S PRAY

Dear God, thanks for creating each of us with extra special abilities.
Help us discover what we're made for and how to use our gifts to help others. In Jesus' name, amen.

54

THE BEST GIFT IS FREE!

God gives us the free gift of life forever in Christ Jesus our Lord.

—*Romans 6:23 ICB*

Out of sheer generosity He put us in right standing with Himself. A pure gift. He got us out of the mess we're in and restored us to where He always wanted us to be. And He did it by means of Jesus Christ.

—*Romans 3:24 THE MESSAGE*

You were saved by faith in God, who treats us much better than we deserve. This is God's gift to you, and not anything you have done on your own. It isn't something you have earned, so there is nothing you can brag about.

—*Ephesians 2:8–9 CEV*

If you declare with your mouth, "Jesus is Lord," and if you believe in your heart that God raised Jesus from death, then you will be saved. We believe with our hearts, and so we are made right with God. And we declare with our mouths to say that we believe, and so we are saved. As the Scripture says, "Anyone who trusts in Him will never be disappointed."

—*Romans 10:9–11 ICB*

LET'S THINK

Surely you've seen one offer or another advertising a "free gift." But there's always a "catch," something you have to do to get that gift. Think through what the Bible says about the "free gift" from God. What is the "free gift"? What is unusual about it?

•••

You've probably heard this saying: "If something seems too good to be true, it probably is (too good to be true)." How do you know that God's gift is not too good to be true? What do we need to do to get it?

LET'S DO

Talk about whether you have accepted God's free gift. If you believe that this "exciting offer is true" and want to accept it, share it!

LET'S PRAY

Dear God, thanks for loving us so much. Thanks for the free gift of eternal life in heaven with You someday. In Jesus' name, amen.

TAKE TEN!

TAKE TURNS LETTING EACH FAMILY MEMBER ANSWER THE QUESTIONS BELOW.

About Others

1. Who do you know would be called "helpful" and why?

2. What do others need that you have to give?

3. How can you encourage others?

About You

4. How do you like to help people and why?

5. What gifts do you have?

6   What have you had to ask for more than once to get?

About Stuff

7   What free gift have you gotten?

8   What godly "superpower" would you like to have and why?

9   How does it feel to share or give things away?

10   What have you received that you were totally surprised to get?

55

VICTORIOUS POWER

Then Moses and the Israelites sang this song to the Lord: "I will sing to the Lord because He is worthy of great honor. He has thrown the horse and its rider into the sea. The Lord gives me strength and makes me sing. He has saved me. He is my God, and I will praise Him. He is the God of my ancestors, and I will honor Him. The Lord is a great warrior. . . . The chariots and soldiers of the king of Egypt He has thrown into the sea. . . . The deep waters covered them. They sank to the bottom like a rock. . . . In Your great victory You destroyed those who were against You. Your anger destroyed them, like fire burning straw. Just a blast of Your breath, and the waters were blown back. The moving water stood up like a wall. And the deep waters became solid in the middle of the sea.

"The enemy bragged, 'I'll chase them and catch them. I'll take all their riches. I'll take all I want. I'll pull out my sword, and my hand will destroy them.' But You blew on them with Your breath and covered them with the sea. They sank like lead in the powerful water.

"Are there any gods like You, Lord? No! There are no gods like You. You are wonderfully holy. You are amazingly powerful. You do great miracles."

—*Exodus 15:1–5, 7–11 ICB*

LET'S THINK

This is the victory song that the Israelites sang after God helped them escape from slavery in Egypt. When they thought they were trapped by the Red Sea, God parted it and they passed through on dry ground! Their Egyptian enemies expected to get through too. But their wheels got stuck in the mud, and the waters closed around them! Note: You can find more of the story in Exodus 14.

...

How did God show His power?
How would you feel toward God if you had been there?
What do you think of God knowing this really happened?

LET'S DO

Talk about how powerful and victorious God is.
Come up with examples from the Bible and today.

LET'S PRAY

Dear God, You are awesome! Thank You for using Your victorious power to save the Israelites and show the Egyptians who is Lord. Thank You for loving us, giving us strength, and rescuing us too. In Jesus' name, amen.

56

AMAZING VICTORY

At the same time, the Philistine was coming closer to David. The man who held his shield walked in front of him. Goliath looked at David. He saw that David was only a boy, tanned and handsome. He looked down at David with disgust. He said, "Do you think I am a dog, that you come at me with a stick?" . . . But David said to him, "You come to me using a sword, a large spear and a small spear. But I come to you in the name of the Lord of heaven's armies. He's the God of the armies of Israel! You have spoken out against Him. Today the Lord will give you to me. . . . Then all the world will know there is a God in Israel! Everyone gathered here will know the Lord does not need swords or spears to save people. The battle belongs to Him! And He will help us defeat all of you." As Goliath came near to attack him, David ran quickly to meet him. He took a stone from his pouch. He put it into his sling and slung it. The stone hit the Philistine on his forehead and sank into it. Goliath fell face down on the ground. So David defeated the Philistine with only a sling and a stone! He hit him and killed him. He did not even have a sword in his hand. . . . When the Philistines saw that their champion was dead, they turned and ran.

—I Samuel 17:41–43, 45–51 ICB

LET'S THINK

Did you know that there was an entire Philistine army ready to attack God's people? They taunted the Israelites for forty days. Their champion fighter, a giant over 9 feet tall, challenged Israel to choose their best warrior to fight him. The losers would become the winner's servants. No one but young David stepped up to the challenge.

•••

How did God use a boy to show His power?
Why do you think David believed he would be victorious?

LET'S DO

Roll call! Time for each family member to shout about how God helped them to be victorious over big (or small) problems.

•••

Come up with a word that describes someone who is strong and courageous. Take turns standing up and saying, "God helps me be. . ."

LET'S PRAY

Dear God, You helped David do awesome things! Please help us do big things too—especially when we are feeling small and unimportant. Thank You for loving us and giving us the strength to do amazing things. In Jesus' name, amen.

57

AMAZING GOD!

Elijah . . . said, "How long will you try to serve both Baal and the Lord? If the Lord is the true God, follow Him. But if Baal is the true God, follow him!"

. . . Elijah said, "...Bring two bulls. Let the prophets of Baal choose one bull. Let them kill it and . . . put the meat on the wood. But they are not to set fire to it. Then I will do the same with the other bull. . . . Pray to your god. And I will pray to the Lord. The god who answers the prayer will set fire to His wood. He is the true God." All the people agreed that this was a good idea.

Then Elijah said to the prophets of Baal, ". . .You go first. . . ."

They prayed to Baal from morning until noon. They shouted, "Baal, answer us!" But there was no sound. No one answered . . . Elijah used [twelve] stones to rebuild the altar in honor of the Lord . . . Elijah put the wood on the altar. . . . Then he said, "Lord, answer my prayer. Show these people that you, Lord, are God . . ."

Then fire from the Lord came down. It burned the sacrifice, the wood, the stones and the ground around the altar. It also dried up the water in the ditch. When all the people saw this, they fell down to the ground. They cried, "The Lord is God! The Lord is God!"

—I Kings 18:21–30, 32–39 ICB

LET'S THINK

Think about what it must have been like to be there!
What do you think the people were thinking?

LET'S DO

Talk about a time or situation where you'd like God
to show His power. Use your imaginations—what would you
like Him to do in that situation?

LET'S PRAY

Dear God, You have done absolutely amazing things! Thank You for
proving Your power again and again. In Jesus' name, amen.

58

THE BLIND SEE!

Jesus was coming near the city of Jericho. There was a blind man sitting beside the road, begging for money. When he heard the people coming down the road, he asked, "What is happening?"

They told him, "Jesus, the One from Nazareth, is coming here."

The blind man cried out, "Jesus, Son of David! Please help me!"

The people who were in front, leading the group, told the blind man to be quiet. But the blind man shouted more and more, "Son of David, please help me!"

Jesus stopped and said, "Bring the blind man to me!" When he came near, Jesus asked him, "What do you want Me to do for you?"

He said, "Lord, I want to see again."

Jesus said to him, "Then see! You are healed because you believed."

At once the man was able to see, and he followed Jesus, thanking God. All the people who saw this praised God.

—Luke 18:35–43 ICB

We have all been told "Enough already," to be quiet or to stop whining. Has anyone told you to stop asking for something? Are you persistent and ask anyway? What is it you want? Have you asked God for it?

...

The blind beggar was initially asking for money. Once he heard it was Jesus who was coming by, he asked for help. Jesus asked him, "What do you want Me to do for you?" Why did Jesus ask that? What do you think about the man's request and response?

...

Think about what you actually want God to do. And ask Him for it.

LET'S DO

Talk about your needs and answered prayers. How have you responded when your prayers were answered?

LET'S PRAY

Dear God, You have done great things! Thank You for using Your healing power to show us who You are. Help us to be specific and ask for the right things. Thank You for loving and caring for us. In Jesus' name, amen.

59

A CHANGE OF HEART

Saul was still trying to frighten the followers of the Lord by saying he would kill them. . . . So Saul went to Damascus. As he came near the city, a bright light from heaven suddenly flashed around him. Saul fell to the ground. He heard a voice saying to him, "Saul, Saul! Why are you doing things against Me?"

Saul said, "Who are you, Lord?"

The voice answered, "I am Jesus. I am the One you are trying to hurt. Get up now and go into the city. Someone there will tell you what you must do."

. . . Saul got up from the ground. He opened his eyes, but he could not see . . .

There was a follower of Jesus in Damascus named Ananias. The Lord spoke to Ananias in a vision . . . [and] said to him, "Get up and . . . find the house of Judas. Ask for a man named Saul . . . I have chosen Saul for an important work. He must tell about Me to non-Jews, to kings, and to the people of Israel."

. . . So Ananias went . . . laid his hands on Saul and said, "Brother Saul, the Lord Jesus sent me. He is the One you saw on the road on your way here. He sent me so that you can see again and be filled with the Holy Spirit."

Immediately, something that looked like fish scales fell from Saul's eyes. He was able to see again! Then Saul got up and was baptized.

—Acts 9:1, 3–12, 15, 17–18 ICB

LET'S THINK

Saul was frightening and killing God's children before the Lord got his attention. God gave Saul new eyes to see that what he was doing was wrong. God changed Saul's heart and sent him on to do important work as a follower of Christ!

...

How will you react the next time someone is mean to you? Will you try to hurt them back or pray for God to open their eyes?

LET'S DO

God had plans for Saul all along! He became the apostle Paul. What are God's plans for you?

...

Silently, pray for someone who has been mean to you. Ask God to open their eyes to see that they need to change.

LET'S PRAY

Dear God, You are awesome! Thank You for getting our attention. Help us see what You want us to do and then do it. We love You. In Jesus' name, amen.

60

YOUR FAITH MADE IT HAPPEN

When Jesus was going into the town of Capernaum, an army officer came up to Him and said, "Lord, my servant is at home in such terrible pain that he can't even move."

"I will go and heal him," Jesus replied.

But the officer said, "Lord, I'm not good enough for You to come into my house. Just give the order, and my servant will get well. I have officers who give orders to me, and I have soldiers who take orders from me. I can say to one of them, 'Go!' and he goes. I can say to another, 'Come!' and he comes. I can say to my servant, 'Do this!' and he will do it."

When Jesus heard this, He was so surprised that he turned and said to the crowd following Him, "I tell you that in all of Israel I've never found anyone with this much faith!" . . .

Then Jesus said to the officer, "You may go home now. Your faith has made it happen."

Right then his servant was healed.

—*Matthew 8:5–10, 13 CEV*

*Jesus didn't need to be physically with the servant
when He healed him. Why not?*

•••

*The crowds did not see the servant get healed,
and neither did the officer. Why do you think that is important?*

•••

*Jesus is not physically here on earth right now.
Do you think He can still heal? Why?*

LET'S DO

*Discuss this topic with your family: Why doesn't God heal everyone?
What is He teaching us through our suffering? Talk about how you
as a family can reach out to someone who is going through a difficult
time, and then follow through!*

•••

*Have you ever found blessings through hardships? A new friendship?
A newfound faith? A new appreciation for someone?*

LET'S PRAY

*Dear God, thank You for Your healing mercies. Give us peace and joy
even when healing is not part of Your plan. We trust You.
In Jesus' name, amen.*

61

ABUNDANT FISHERMEN

[Jesus] said to Simon, "Take the boat into deep water. If you will put your nets in the water, you will catch some fish."

Simon answered, "Master, we worked hard all night trying to catch fish, but we caught nothing. But You say to put the nets in the water; so I will." The fishermen did as Jesus told them. And they caught so many fish that the nets began to break. They called to their friends in the other boat to come and help them. The friends came, and both boats were filled so full that they were almost sinking.

The fishermen were all amazed at the many fish they caught. When Simon Peter saw what had happened, he bowed down before Jesus and said, "Go away from me, Lord. I am a sinful man!" James and John, the sons of Zebedee, were amazed too. (James and John were Simon's partners.)

Jesus said to Simon, "Don't be afraid. From now on you will be fishermen for men." When the men brought their boats to the shore, they left everything and followed Jesus.

—Luke 5:4–11 ICB

LET'S THINK

*Why do you think they hadn't caught fish all night—and why would
Jesus tell them to try again? Do you wonder why would He fill the nets
that much? And why did Simon Peter respond as he did?
Why would Jesus tell them not to be afraid?*

•••

*The fact that the men left everything to follow Jesus and be
"fishermen for men" may seem strange if you do not know the rest of
their story. Jesus called them to be His disciples, to learn from Him and
tell others about His saving power. How is the fact that
"we were told" a miracle too?*

LET'S DO

*Roll call! Ask each family member to answer the following questions:
How did you find out about Jesus?
How can you share Jesus with others?*

LET'S PRAY

*Dear God, it is amazing, how much You love us. You have done
miracles to prove it! Help us share the Good News with others too.
In Jesus' name, amen.*

62

GOT TIME FOR FOOD?

When Jesus arrived, He saw a large crowd. He felt sorry for them and healed those who were sick. Late that afternoon, His followers came to Jesus and said, "No one lives in this place. And it is already late. Send the people away so they can go to the towns and buy food for themselves."

Jesus answered, "They don't need to go away. You give them some food to eat."

The followers answered, "But we have only five loaves of bread and two fish."

Jesus said, "Bring the bread and the fish to Me." Then He told the people to sit down on the grass. He took the five loaves of bread and the two fish. Then He looked to heaven and thanked God for the food. Jesus divided the loaves of bread. He gave them to His followers, and they gave the bread to the people. All the people ate and were satisfied.

After they finished eating, the followers filled twelve baskets with the pieces of food that were not eaten. There were about five thousand men there who ate, as well as women and children.

—Matthew 14:14–21 ICB

As soon as Jesus arrived on shore, He felt compassion for the large crowd. What was Jesus doing before His followers thought to send the people away to eat?

•••

Think about the amazing things Jesus must have done earlier that day. Why do you think His followers wanted to "take a break" from healing the sick? What did Jesus say about that idea? Do you think He was setting it up for a bigger miracle, or was He showing them that He cared?

LET'S DO

As a family, come up with a big idea on how to help others and then start planning to make it happen. Ask God to guide you in your efforts.

LET'S PRAY

Dear God, You have done miraculous things! Thank You for helping us with big things and small things. Thank You for loving us and caring for us. In Jesus' name, amen.

63

FREEDOM!

After being severely beaten, Paul and Silas were thrown into jail. The jailer was ordered to guard them carefully. When he heard this order, he put them far inside the jail. He pinned down their feet between large blocks of wood.

About midnight Paul and Silas were praying and singing songs to God. The other prisoners were listening to them. Suddenly, there was a big earthquake. It was so strong that it shook the foundation of the jail. Then all the doors of the jail broke open. All the prisoners were freed from their chains. The jailer woke up and saw that the jail doors were open. He thought that the prisoners had already escaped. So he got his sword and was about to kill himself. But Paul shouted, "Don't hurt yourself! We are all here!"

The jailer told someone to bring a light. Then he ran inside. Shaking with fear, he fell down before Paul and Silas. Then he brought them outside and said, "Men, what must I do to be saved?"

They said to him, "Believe in the Lord Jesus and you will be saved—you and all the people in your house." So Paul and Silas told the message of the Lord to the jailer and all the people in his house. . . . He and his family were very happy because they now believed in God.

—Acts 16:23–32, 34 ICB

LET'S THINK

Paul and Silas ended up in jail because they shared about God's saving love to people who did not want to hear it. Do you think they gave up? No, even in chains, Paul and Silas were praying and singing praises to God!

•••

Would you consider what happened next to be a miracle? Why? Why do you think the jailer changed to being "one of them"? Would you consider that a miracle? Why?

LET'S DO

Did you know missionaries live all over the world? Pull out a globe or a map of the world online and have each family member close their eyes as they place their finger on the map. Wherever the fingers land, pray for the missionaries in that country.

LET'S PRAY

Dear God, You do miraculous things! Please help us and the missionaries in dangerous places to spread the Good News about Your saving love. In Jesus' name, amen.

TAKE TEN!

TAKE TURNS LETTING EACH FAMILY MEMBER ANSWER THE QUESTIONS BELOW.

About Others

1. Do you know someone who God has helped do amazing things?

2. What have others done to help you know God?

3. How can you help others know God?

About You

4. Why do you think God is amazing?

5 What is one of your favorite, "most awesome" Bible stories?

6 What is one of your favorite praise songs?

About Stuff

7 What crazy thing has happened that must have had God behind it?

8 What cool things in nature prove to you that there is a God?

9 How has God provided for you?

10 What kind of miracle would you like to see?

64

ONE GOD

Obey the things I command you today. . . . Don't worship any other god. This is because I, the Lord, the Jealous One, am a jealous God.

—Exodus 34:11, 14 ICB

Who may go up on the mountain of the Lord?
  Who may stand in His holy Temple?
Only those with clean hands and pure hearts.
  They must not have worshiped idols.
  They must not have made promises in the name of a false god.
It is they who will receive a blessing from the Lord.
  The God who saves them will declare them right.

—Psalm 24:3–5 ICB

After the Philistines had captured the ark of God, they took it from Ebenezer to Ashdod, brought it into the temple of Dagon and placed it next to his statue. When the people of Ashdod got up early the next morning, there was Dagon, fallen with his face to the ground before the ark of the LORD. So they took Dagon and returned him to his place. But when they got up early the next morning, there was Dagon, fallen with his face to the ground before the ark of the LORD. This time, Dagon's head and both of his hands were broken off and lying on the threshold. Only Dagon's torso remained.

—I Samuel 5:1–4 CSB

148

David writes about blessings to those who worship the Lord and no one else. That rule is at the top of the Ten Commandments, which were written on stone tablets stored in the Ark of the Covenant of God. When the Ark was stolen by the Philistines, they put the captured Ark next to a statue of their false god, Dagon, in Dagon's temple.

...

How did the people of Ashdod find the statute of Dagon the first time? The second time? Think about the three passages of today's devotion and how they tie together. Do you think God has a sense of humor? Why?

LET'S DO

Write down some "things" that are important to your family. What extracurricular activities are you involved in? Who is important to your life? Write down everything that means something to you and then number those items in order of importance (and be sure to write God at the top). Post your list as a reminder!

LET'S PRAY

Dear God, the Bible tells us that You are a jealous God and we should love nothing more than You. Help us put You first. Thanks for loving us so much, sending Jesus to save us and make us right with You. In Jesus' name, amen.

65

NUMBER ONE

"I am the A and the Z, the Beginning and the Ending of all things," says God, who is the Lord, the All Powerful One who is, and was, and is coming again!

—*Revelation 1:8 TLB*

No one has seen God, but Jesus is exactly like Him. Christ ranks higher than all the things that have been made. Through His power all things were made—things in heaven and on earth, things seen and unseen, all powers, authorities, lords, and rulers . . . And all things continue because of Him. He is the head of the body. (The body is the church.) Everything comes from Him. And He is the first one who was raised from death. So in all things Jesus is most important.

—*Colossians 1:15–18 ICB*

And you will know that God's power is very great for us who believe. That power is the same as the great strength God used to raise Christ from death and put Him at His right side in heaven . . . Christ is more important than anything in this world or in the next world. God put everything under His power. And God made Him the head over everything for the church.

—*Ephesians 1:19–22 ICB*

LET'S THINK

Christians serve an all-powerful God. He is number one over all the heavens and earth. What words can you find that describe how great God is? How do you feel, knowing who is "number one"?

···

Think about the expressions "Look out for number one" and "You have to take care of yourself because no one else will." They're not talking about God. They're talking about ourselves. What does Matthew tell us that contradicts these phrases?

LET'S DO

Come up with a priority list for your family. What are some values you'd like to prioritize for the weeks ahead? Perhaps becoming slow to anger, quick to listen? Finding new, fresh ways to share Jesus with others? Speaking kind words to one another? Whatever they may be, write them down and strive to enact them.

LET'S PRAY

Dear God, help us remember that You are the most important Being in the universe! Thank You that we are important to You and that You care for us and give us what we need. In Jesus' name, amen.

66

ONE WAY

There is one Lord, one faith, and one baptism. There is one God and Father of everything. He rules everything. He is everywhere and in everything.

—*Ephesians 4:5–6 ICB*

Now we can know God, the One who is true. And our lives are in that true God and in His Son, Jesus Christ. He is the true God, and He is eternal life.

—*I John 5:20 ICB*

God wants all people to be saved. And He wants everyone to know the truth. There is only one God. And there is only one way that people can reach God. That way is through Jesus Christ, who . . . gave Himself to pay for the sins of all people.

—*I Timothy 2:4–6 ICB*

Eternal life is to know You, the only true God, and to know Jesus Christ, the One You sent.

—*John 17:3 CEV*

Jesus answered, "I am the way. And I am the truth and the life. The only way to the Father is through Me."

—*John 14:6 ICB*

LET'S THINK

There are a variety of beliefs in the world today. God's Word tells us repeatedly that there is only One way that is true. What is that One way He wants all people to know? How did Jesus pay for the sins of all people? How do you suppose all people will find the truth?

LET'S DO

Where can we look to find out more about the One true God?

•••

Roll call! Time for every family member to name three things that are true about God.

LET'S PRAY

Dear God, thank You for being our One true God. You want all people to know how very much You love them! Help us remember that You love every one of us and want us to know You.
In Jesus' name, amen.

67

WORSHIP THE LORD!

The time is coming when the true worshipers will worship the Father in spirit and truth. That time is now here. And these are the kinds of worshipers the Father wants. God is spirit. Those who worship God must worship in spirit and truth.

—*John 4:23–24 ICB*

So brothers, since God has shown us great mercy, I beg you to offer your lives as a living sacrifice to Him. Your offering must be only for God and pleasing to Him. This is the spiritual way for you to worship.

—*Romans 12:1 ICB*

Peter began to speak: "I really understand now that to God every person is the same. God accepts anyone who worships Him and does what is right. It is not important what country a person comes from."

—*Acts 10:34–35 ICB*

People everywhere will remember and will turn to the Lord. All the families of the nations will worship Him. This is because the Lord is King. He rules the nations.

—*Psalm 22:27–28 ICB*

Worship is paying homage. That's a word we don't use often. Homage is reverence, honor, and respect. It means being in awe— knowing that God is awesome! God is worthy of praise.

•••

What do you think it means to worship God? Think about who should be worshipping God. What makes people of different nations the same? How do we worship with our bodies and our spirits? Why is God awesome? Look for words that describe God and think of more of your own.

LET'S DO

Talk first about why we should worship God and then about the many different ways we can worship God.

•••

Sing a "worship song" together. Use the internet to help with music and lyrics, or simply take turns telling God why He is awesome.

LET'S PRAY

Dear God, the Bible tells us that You are most holy and glorious. Help us be in awe of You! You are the greatest! Thank You for loving us no matter where we are from. In Jesus' name, amen.

68

PRAISE THE LORD!

Praise the Lord! Praise the Lord from the heavens. Praise Him high above the earth. Praise Him, all you angels. Praise Him, all you armies of heaven. Praise Him, sun and moon. Praise Him, all you shining stars. Praise Him, highest heavens and you waters above the sky. Let them praise the Lord because they were created by His command. He set them in place forever and ever. He made a law that will never end . . . Praise Him, you wild animals and all cattle, small crawling animals and birds. Praise Him, you kings of the earth and all nations, princes and all rulers of the earth. Praise Him, you young men and women, old people and children. Praise the Lord. He alone is great. He is greater than heaven and earth.

—Psalm 148:1–13 ICB

[The crowd] began shouting praise to God for all the powerful works they had seen. They said, "God bless the king who comes in the name of the Lord!

. . . Some of the Pharisees said to Jesus, "Teacher, tell Your followers not to say these things!"

But Jesus answered, "I tell you, if My followers don't say these things, then the stones will cry out."

—Luke 19:37–40 ICB

LET'S THINK

David, who wrote this psalm, gives reasons for praising God. What are they?

•••

As Jesus rode a donkey into Jerusalem, the crowds were happy! They recognized Jesus for who He was and is. What do you think about Jesus' response to the religious leaders?

LET'S DO

Roll call! Time for every family member to think of three things to praise God for.

•••

Take turns jumping up and saying, "Praise God for. . ."

LET'S PRAY

Dear God, the Bible tells us that You are worthy of all praise. Help us rejoice in all You have done! Praise You, Father. Bless You, Jesus. You are great! In Jesus' name, amen.

69

SING TO THE LORD!

Sing to Him. Sing praises to Him. Tell about all the wonderful things He has done.

—I Chronicles 16:9 ICB

You are the LORD's people. Obey Him and celebrate! He deserves your praise. Praise the LORD with harps! Use harps with ten strings to make music for Him. Sing a new song. Shout! Play beautiful music.

—Psalm 33:1–3 CEV

Clap your hands, all you people. Shout to God with joy. The Lord Most High is wonderful. He is the great King over all the earth! . . . Sing praises to God . . . God is King of all the earth. So sing a song of praise to Him. . . . He is supreme.

—Psalm 47:1–2, 6–7, 9 ICB

Everything on earth, shout with joy to God! . . . Make His praise glorious! Say to God, "Your works are amazing! Your power is great. Your enemies fall before You. All the earth worships You."
—Psalm 66:1–4 ICB

Sing psalms, hymns, and spiritual songs with thankfulness in your hearts to God.
—Colossians 3:16 ICB

LET'S THINK

When we are happy and full of joy, our hearts want to burst into song! God brings us joy and deserves our praises. However, every day isn't a musical. We don't usually spontaneously burst into song and dance right where we are. But that doesn't mean we couldn't! Think about things God has done that deserve our praise. If your life were a musical, when would you burst into song?

LET'S DO

We are told at least five hundred times in the Bible to sing, dance, play music, and worship the Lord. Let's do it! Sing or listen to a worship song together. Use the internet to help with music and lyrics. Get up and dance! Clap your hands! Shout out to God! It's okay to feel silly. God loves it when we do what He asks!

LET'S PRAY

Dear God, the Bible tells us to sing, dance, play music, and clap our hands as worship You. Help us be thankful for all You have done! You are the best. In Jesus' name, amen.

70

OUR FATHER

When you pray, you should go into your room and close the door. Then pray to your Father who cannot be seen. Your Father can see what is done in secret, and He will reward you.

And when you pray, don't be like those people who don't know God. They continue saying things that mean nothing. They think that God will hear them because of the many things they say. Don't be like them. Your Father knows the things you need before you ask Him. So when you pray, you should pray like this:

"Our Father in heaven, we pray that Your name will always be kept holy. We pray that Your kingdom will come. We pray that what You want will be done, here on earth as it is in heaven. Give us the food we need for each day. Forgive the sins we have done, just as we have forgiven those who did wrong to us. And do not cause us to be tested; but save us from the Evil One. [The kingdom, the power, and the glory are yours forever. Amen.]"

—*Matthew 6:6–13 ICB*

LET'S THINK

If you have ever wondered how to pray, here it is! Jesus Himself tells us how. For starters, where should we pray? Why? Why does He tell us not to use empty words and phrases and repeat things?

...

Jesus explains the right way to talk to God. Look at each part. Break it down and think carefully about each phrase and what it means.

LET'S DO

Talk about what each part of the Lord's Prayer means in your own words. What should we be asking for and where? What do we need besides food? God does not tempt us (James 1:13–15) but He gives us strength so that when we are tested, we will be able to escape (I Corinthians 10:13). The Lord is our protection and saves those who know Him (Psalm 91:9–16). Why would Jesus want us to remember that God is the most powerful King forever?

LET'S PRAY

Instead of our short prayer, sincerely pray the Lord's Prayer (Matthew 6:9-13).

71

PRAY FOR WHOM?

First, I tell you to pray for all people. Ask God for the things people need, and be thankful to Him. You should pray for kings and for all who have authority. Pray for the leaders so that we can have quiet and peaceful lives—lives full of worship and respect for God. This is good, and it pleases God our Savior.

—I Timothy 2:1–3 ICB

Confess your sins to each other and pray for each other. Do this so that God can heal you. When a good man prays, great things happen.

—James 5:16 ICB

Pray for peace in Jerusalem: "May those who love her be safe. May there be peace within her walls and safety within her strong towers."

—Psalm 122:6–7 ICB

Brothers, the thing I want most is for all the Jews to be saved. That is my prayer to God.

—Romans 10:1 ICB

But I tell you, love your enemies. Pray for those who hurt you.

—Matthew 5:44 ICB

LET'S THINK

*Have you wondered who and what to pray for other than yourself
and your needs? While there's nothing wrong with praying for
yourself (in fact the Bible tells us to do it in Ephesians 6:18), let's take
some time to think about others today. Who does the Bible tell us to
pray for? Is it easier to pray for yourself than for those who hurt you?*

...

*Some of today's Scriptures may surprise you. Use them to help you
think of other people or things to pray for that you normally don't.*

LET'S DO

*Have each family member jot down a list of who they want to pray for.
Then either pray for each person on each list as a group or have quiet
time to pray for them individually.*

LET'S PRAY

*Dear God, we pray for all people. Please give wisdom to our leaders
and peace on earth. We ask that You provide for the needs of our
family, friends, and even for the people who hurt us.
In Jesus' name, amen.*

72

HE HEARS OUR PRAYERS

Never stop praying, especially for others. Always pray by the power of the Spirit. Stay alert and keep praying for God's people. Pray that I will be given the message to speak and that I may fearlessly explain the mystery about the Good News. I was sent to do this work, and that's the reason I am in jail. So pray that I will be brave and will speak as I should.

—*Ephesians 6:18–20 CEV*

Always be happy. Never stop praying. Give thanks whatever happens. That is what God wants for you in Christ Jesus.

—*I Thessalonians 5:16–18 ICB*

All of you who fear God, come and listen. I will tell you what He has done for me. I cried out to Him with my mouth. I praised Him with my tongue. If I had known of any sin in my heart, the Lord would not have listened to me. But God has listened. He has heard my prayer. Praise God. He did not ignore my prayer. He did not hold back His love from me.

—*Psalm 66:16–20 ICB*

LET'S THINK

Have you ever wondered whether it is worth it to keep praying? Today's Scriptures should encourage us not to give up! What encouraging words can you find in them?

•••

Paul tells the Ephesians to pray for God's people and himself. Why did Paul need prayer? Who do you know that could use those same prayers like Paul? Why?

•••

David is writing about his relationship with God in Psalm 66. What can we learn from David's experiences? How do you personally relate . . . and how can you share with others what God has done for you?

LET'S DO

Talk about what it means to never stop praying.

•••

Roll call! Time for every family member to come up with a unique way to remind themselves to pray throughout the day. (Maybe write the word "prayer" at the top of your planner—or make it a habit to pray before meals. What other things can you think of?)

LET'S PRAY

Dear God, thank You for listening to us all the time. Help us remember that You are always there for us and hear our prayers. Thanks for loving us. Help us share Your love with others. In Jesus' name, amen.

TAKE TEN!

TAKE TURNS LETTING EACH FAMILY MEMBER ANSWER THE QUESTIONS BELOW.

About Others

1   Do you know someone who is struggling right now at this moment?

2   Who can you continue to pray for?

3   How can you help others find the one true God?

About You

4   What is one of your favorite praise and worship songs and why?

5 What do you see every day that shows God's power?

6 What makes you the most animated and excited about God and what He's done?

About Stuff

7 What can become more important than God?

8 Taking turns, can you say the entire Lord's Prayer from memory?

9 How has God answered one of your prayers?

10 What makes you want to jump up and praise the Lord?

73

WHICH WAY IS RIGHT?

Your word is like a lamp for my feet and a light for my way.

—*Psalm 119:105 ICB*

Listen, people of Israel! The Lord is our God. He is the only Lord. Love the Lord your God with all your heart, soul and strength. Always remember these commands I give you today. Teach them to your children. Talk about them when you sit at home and walk along the road. Talk about them when you lie down and when you get up. Write them down and tie them to your hands as a sign. Tie them on your forehead to remind you. Write them on your doors and gates.

—Deuteronomy 6:4–9 ICB

I treasure Your Word above all else; it keeps me from sinning against You.

—*Psalm 119:11 CEV*

Make them [My disciples] pure and holy through teaching them Your words of truth.

—*John 17:17 TLB*

LET'S THINK

We often wonder what to do. Which way is right? What does God want us to do? Where can we go to find out?

...

"These commands" mentioned in Deuteronomy are the Ten Commandments. They are found in the chapter right before these verses. God's words are not some ancient text that we cannot continue to learn from. What do God's words do for us? How do they affect our soul and spirit? And what does that even mean? Hint: think about what we humans want versus what God wants.

LET'S DO

Since God's Word is the lamp to our feet, come up with three Scriptures for your family to focus on in the days and weeks ahead. Write them down! Maybe even challenge each other to memorize them. Scripture is a "treasure" in and of itself, but maybe an "earthly treasure" would give you incentive. What could it be?

LET'S PRAY

Dear God, thank You for the direction You give us through the Bible. Help us understand it and use it in our life, especially when we have tough decisions to make. We love You. In Jesus' name, amen.

74

SEE THE LIGHT

The Good News that we preach may be hidden. But it is hidden only to those who are lost. . . . They cannot see the light of the Good News—the Good News about the glory of Christ, who is exactly like God. . . . God once said, "Let the light shine out of the darkness!" And this is the same God who made His light shine in our hearts. He gave us light by letting us know the glory of God that is in the face of Christ.

—II Corinthians 4:3–4, 6 ICB

Later, Jesus talked to the people again. He said, "I am the light of the world. The person who follows Me will never live in darkness. He will have the light that gives life."

—John 8:12 ICB

You are the light that gives light to the world. A city that is built on a hill cannot be hidden. And people don't hide a light under a bowl. They put the light on a lampstand. Then the light shines for all the people in the house. In the same way, you should be a light for other people. Live so that they will see the good things you do. Live so that they will praise your Father in heaven.

—Matthew 5:14–16 ICB

The idiom "to see the light" means to understand something that was not previously understood. Do you think this saying came from these Scriptures? What is that "Light" or "Good News" we need to see? How can we show it to others?

...

Paul wrote, "God once said, 'Let the light shine out of the darkness!' And this is the same God who made His light shine in our hearts." What do you think Paul means? How does, "Let there be light!" (Genesis 1:3) relate with the light of the Good News? How can we live like a light?

LET'S DO

As a family, come up with unique ways to share God's light. Perhaps volunteer at a local nonprofit, offer to host a dinner party, or sign up for a mission trip together.

...

Getting along with everyone can be hard sometimes. How can you shine His light when you are frustrated with others?

LET'S PRAY

Dear God, thank You for sending the Light into this dark world. Help us see the Light, know the Light, and share the Light with others. In Jesus' name, amen.

75

BELIEVING HEARTS

But this is what the Scripture says about being made right through faith. . . . "God's teaching is near you; it is in your mouth and in your heart." That is the teaching of faith that we tell. If you declare with your mouth, "Jesus is Lord," and if you believe in your heart that God raised Jesus from death, then you will be saved. We believe with our hearts, and so we are made right with God. And we declare with our mouths to say that we believe, and so we are saved. As the Scripture says, "Anyone who trusts in Him will never be disappointed." . . . The same Lord is the Lord of all and gives many blessings to all who trust in Him. The Scripture says, "Anyone who asks the Lord for help will be saved."

—*Romans 10:6, 8–13 ICB*

Anyone who belongs to Christ is a new person. The past is forgotten, and everything is new.

—*II Corinthians 5:17 CEV*

You believe in God through Christ. God raised Christ from death and gave Him glory. So your faith and your hope are in God. . . . You have been born again. This new life did not come from something that dies, but from something that cannot die. You were born again through God's living message that continues forever.

—*I Peter 1:21, 23 ICB*

LET'S THINK

Scripture tells us how to be made right with God through faith. What does faith mean?

...

Some questions to discuss: What does it mean to "be made right" or "be a new person" or "born again"? Who can be saved? What do we need to do with our mouths, in our hearts?

LET'S DO

Do you believe that Jesus is Lord and God raised Him from the dead? If so, say together, out loud, "I believe!"

LET'S PRAY

Dear God, thank You for giving us hearts to believe and mouths to declare that You are Lord. Thank You for loving us so much and for forgiving our sins so that we can start over—new in Christ. We love You. In Jesus' name, amen.

76

JOY, PEACE, AND PATIENCE

Do your best to improve your faith. You can do this by adding goodness, understanding, self-control, patience, devotion to God, concern for others, and love. If you keep growing in this way, it will show that what you know about our Lord Jesus Christ has made your lives useful and meaningful.

—II Peter 1:5–8 CEV

We have been made right with God because of our faith. So we have peace with God through our Lord Jesus Christ. Through our faith, Christ has brought us into that blessing of God's grace that we now enjoy. And we are happy because of the hope we have of sharing God's glory. And we also have joy with our troubles because we know that these troubles produce patience. And patience produces character, and character produces hope. And this hope will never disappoint us, because God has poured out His love to fill our hearts. God gave us His love through the Holy Spirit, whom God has given to us.

—Romans 5:1–5 ICB

Dear friends, keep building on the foundation of your most holy faith, as the Holy Spirit helps you to pray. And keep in step with God's love, as you wait for our Lord Jesus Christ to show how kind He is by giving you eternal life.

—Jude 1:20–21 CEV

LET'S THINK

God loves us through our faith journeys no matter where we are on that path. What do Christ-followers need to do in order to make their lives more useful and meaningful?

...

Faith in God gives us peace in our eternal future, but what does it give us now? What should make Christians happy? Why should Christ-followers have joy even during troubles? How do troubles produce patience? Why does patience produce character? And since character produces hope, we have come full circle—because that hope is in God—and His love seals the deal. We will not be disappointed.

LET'S DO

Patience is sometimes hard when it comes to family. It's almost easier to be more patient with a total stranger on the street than it is with our very own sibling. Discuss this as a family and come up with examples of how we can practice patience with each other.

LET'S PRAY

Dear God, thanks for loving us so much. Help us keep the faith and grow in our understanding of You. Give us meaning and purpose. In Jesus' name, amen.

77

ROOTED IN HIM

People who are evil and cheat other people will go from bad to worse. They will fool others, but they will also be fooling themselves. But you should continue following the teachings that you learned. You know that these teachings are true. And you know you can trust those who taught you. You have known the Holy Scriptures since you were a child. The Scriptures are able to make you wise. And that wisdom leads to salvation through faith in Christ Jesus.

—*II Timothy 3:13–15 ICB*

Dear friends, you already know about this. So be careful. Do not let those evil people lead you away by the wrong they do. Be careful so that you will not fall from your own strong faith. But grow in the grace and knowledge of our Lord and Savior Jesus Christ. Glory be to Him now and forever! Amen.

—*II Peter 3:17–18 ICB*

As you received Christ Jesus the Lord, so continue to live in Him. Keep your roots deep in Him and have your lives built on Him. Be strong in the faith, just as you were taught. And always be thankful. Be sure that no one leads you away with false ideas and words that mean nothing. Those ideas come from men. They are the worthless ideas of this world. They are not from Christ.

—*Colossians 2:6–8 ICB*

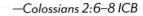

LET'S THINK

Be careful out there! We can be tricked into believing that good things are bad and bad things are good.

•••

What things are promoted as good that are actually bad according to the Bible? What do we need to do to prevent ourselves from getting confused? Where can we get godly wisdom?

LET'S DO

Adults, what do you wish you had known when you were kids or teenagers? Take a moment to jot down some advice to "your younger self."

•••

Kids/teens, what tough situations have you found yourself in? How did you know what was the right or wrong thing to do? Share your thoughts with the rest of the family.

LET'S PRAY

Dear God, help us keep the faith and learn more about You every day by reading Your Word. Show us right from wrong and when we are being tricked. Keep us on the right track. We love You. In Jesus' name, amen.

78

LOVE LIKE JESUS

Don't be proud but accept God's teaching that is planted in your hearts. This teaching can save your souls. Do what God's teaching says; do not just listen and do nothing. When you only sit and listen, you are fooling yourselves. A person who hears God's teaching and does nothing is like a man looking in a mirror. He sees his face, then goes away and quickly forgets what he looked like. But the truly happy person is the one who carefully studies God's perfect law that makes people free. He continues to study it. He listens to God's teaching and does not forget what he heard. Then he obeys what God's teaching says. When he does this, it makes him happy.

—James 1:21–25 ICB

My brothers, if someone says he has faith, but does nothing, his faith is worth nothing. Can faith like that save him? A brother or sister in Christ might need clothes or might need food. And you say to him, "God be with you! I hope you stay warm and get plenty to eat." You say this, but you do not give that person the things he needs. Unless you help him, your words are worth nothing. It is the same with faith. If faith does nothing, then that faith is dead, because it is alone.

—James 2:14–17 ICB

LET'S THINK

Have you heard the expression "Bible fatheads"? They are people who fill their mind with all kinds of Bible information and are ready to beat their opponents mentally, as if life is some sort of TV game show. They know but they don't do. Where can we find what we should do?

•••

Christians are sometimes criticized because they don't follow Jesus' teachings. They are called hypocrites or "holier than thou." Think about what the Bible has to say about that. How can Christ-followers be more like Christ? Why is this important?

LET'S DO

Talk about what Christians do that is right.
Talk about what Christians do wrong.

•••

What can your family do right?

LET'S PRAY

Dear God, thanks for reminding us to do what You want us to. Help us to learn from the Bible, see opportunities to do right, and do them. Help us to be more like Christ and love others like You love us.
In Jesus' name, amen.

79

KEEP THE FAITH!

And let us not get tired of doing what is right, for after a while we will reap a harvest of blessing if we don't get discouraged and give up.

—*Galatians 6:9 TLB*

Dear friends, keep building on the foundation of your most holy faith, as the Holy Spirit helps you to pray. And keep in step with God's love, as you wait for our Lord Jesus Christ to show how kind He is by giving you eternal life.

—*Jude 1:20–21 CEV*

Let us hold firmly to the hope that we have confessed. We can trust God to do what He promised. Let us think about each other and help each other to show love and do good deeds. You should not stay away from the church meetings, as some are doing. But you should meet together and encourage each other. Do this even more as you see the Day coming.

—*Hebrews 10:23–25 ICB*

. . .We should wear faith and love to protect us. And the hope of salvation should be our helmet. God. . .choose us. . .to have salvation through our Lord Jesus Christ. Jesus died for us so that we can live together with Him. . . . So comfort each other and give each other strength, just as you are doing now.

—*I Thessalonians 5:8–11 ICB*

LET'S THINK

The Bible offers Christ-followers encouragement and hope
for great rewards. Think about those rewards. What are they?
How can we protect and encourage ourselves?
How can we be an encouragement to others?

LET'S DO

Pass out blank greeting cards, notepads, pens, and paper, and invite
each family member to write an encouraging note to someone who
could use a little pick-me-up. Share them in person or send them in
the mail. Let the recipients know that they are loved and that you are
praying for them!

LET'S PRAY

Dear God, thanks for encouragers. Help us be an encouragement to
others in their faith. In Jesus' name, amen.

GOD'S AWESOME POWER

Finally, let the mighty strength of the Lord make you strong. Put on all the armor that God gives, so you can defend yourself against the devil's tricks. We are not fighting against humans. We are fighting against forces and authorities and against rulers of darkness and powers in the spiritual world. So put on all the armor that God gives. Then when that evil day comes, you will be able to defend yourself. And when the battle is over, you will still be standing firm. Be ready! Let the truth be like a belt around your waist, and let God's justice protect you like armor. Your desire to tell the good news about peace should be like shoes on your feet. Let your faith be like a shield, and you will be able to stop all the flaming arrows of the evil one. Let God's saving power be like a helmet, and for a sword use God's message that comes from the Spirit.

—*Ephesians 6:10–17 CEV*

My dear children, you belong to God. So you have defeated them because God's Spirit, who is in you, is greater than the devil, who is in the world.

—*I John 4:4 ICB*

I can do all things through Christ because He gives me strength.

—*Philippians 4:13 ICB*

Most superheroes are ordinary people—good guys who have super-powers to help them defeat bad guys. Think about how Christians are ordinary good guys. What superpower do they have? What protection does God give?

...

Think about a sword. A sword is not only a weapon used for defense but is used on the offense too. Think about the other pieces of protective gear in Ephesians and what they do. How do they symbolically match each need for protection?

...

Why is it important to know Scripture? What do Christ-followers need to hold strong against? Why are Christians going to win?

LET'S DO

Discussion topic: have each family member talk about a time when God's superpowers showed up in their lives.

LET'S PRAY

Dear God, thanks for protecting us. Because of You and Your Word, we have a full body of armor. Help us to know when and where to raise our shield. Help us remember what is in Your Word so we can stand up and fight. In Jesus' name, amen.

81

GOD NEVER LEAVES US

We have this treasure from God. But we are only like clay jars that hold the treasure. This shows that this great power is from God, not from us. We have troubles all around us, but we are not defeated. We do not know what to do, but we do not give up. We are persecuted, but God does not leave us. We are hurt sometimes, but we are not destroyed. We carry the death of Jesus in our own bodies, so that the life of Jesus can also be seen in our bodies. . . . It is written in the Scriptures, "I believed, so I spoke." Our faith is like this, too. We believe, and so we speak . . . so the grace of God is being given to more and more people. . . . So we do not give up. . . . We have small troubles for a while now, but they are helping us gain an eternal glory.

—II Corinthians 4:7–10, 13, 15–17 ICB

I have fought the good fight. I have finished the race. I have kept the faith. Now, a crown is waiting for me. I will get that crown for being right with God.

—II Timothy 4:7–8 ICB

LET'S THINK

Think about the lyrics, "Jesus loves me, this I know, for the Bible tells me so. Little ones to Him belong; they are weak but He is strong." How does Paul's message to the Corinthians match where children can find strength? Why is it important that we know where the power comes from?

•••

Today we get ribbons or trophies, but in Paul's day, people got a crown for crossing the finish line. What is the reward for being right with God all the way to the end?

LET'S DO

Roll call! Time for every family member to name three things that could stop people from believing and sharing what they know about Jesus.

•••

Now, take turns talking about what we can do to gain strength and remain faithful to God.

LET'S PRAY

Dear God, help us not give up when we feel weak and helpless. Thank You for the crown that awaits us. In Jesus' name, amen.

TAKE TEN!

TAKE TURNS LETTING EACH FAMILY MEMBER ANSWER THE QUESTIONS BELOW.

About Others

1. What makes someone real rather than a "phony" or "fake" hypocrite?

2. Who is a good example of a faithful follower of Christ and why?

3. How has someone shown their faith with their actions?

About You

4. What are some of the best ways to help you learn Scripture?

5 What helps or helped grow your faith?

6 What have you done this week that Jesus would be proud of?

About Stuff

7 How do we know right from wrong?

8 How do we know what we believe?

9 How has God helped someone you know when they were scared or discouraged?

10 What keeps you going when you feel like quitting?

82

HE BRINGS GOOD NEWS

But before people can trust in the Lord for help, they must believe in Him. And before they can believe in the Lord, they must hear about Him. And for them to hear about the Lord, someone must tell them. And before someone can go and tell them, he must be sent. It is written, "How beautiful is the person who comes to bring good news."

—*Romans 10:14–15 ICB*

How beautiful is the person who comes over the mountains to bring good news. How beautiful is the one who announces peace. He brings good news and announces salvation. How beautiful are the feet of the one who says to Jerusalem, "Your God is King."

—*Isaiah 52:7 ICB*

Jesus traveled through all the towns and villages. He taught in their synagogues and told people the Good News about the kingdom. And He healed all kinds of diseases and sicknesses. He saw the crowds of people and felt sorry for them because they were worried and helpless. They were like sheep without a shepherd. Jesus said to His followers, "There are many people to harvest, but there are only a few workers to help harvest them. God owns the harvest. Pray to Him that He will send more workers to help gather His harvest."

—*Matthew 9:35–38 ICB*

LET'S THINK

*Who is bringing the "Good News" in each of today's Scriptures?
To whom are they bringing it?*

...

*A familiar Christmas carol starts, "Go, tell it on the mountain, over
the hills and everywhere, that Jesus Christ is born." Jesus' being born
is the start of the New Testament, the "second half" of the story.
What is the rest of the Good News that Jesus brings us?*

LET'S DO

*God used shepherds to spread the Good News about Jesus.
Jesus became poor and lowly when He came to earth to tell poor,
lowly followers the Good News. Those followers told many people;
those people told people, who told people . . . who eventually told us!
Most of us are ordinary people too.*

...

*Write down everyone's talents in the family and come up with a plan to
reach people with the Good News that only your family can do.*

LET'S PRAY

*Dear God, thank You for sending angels to announce Jesus, the Good
News of salvation, and also for His disciples who helped spread the
Good News. Show us how to help You too. In Jesus' name, amen.*

83

BE MY PROOF

To Theophilus,

The first book I wrote was about everything that Jesus did and taught. I wrote about the whole life of Jesus, from the beginning until the day He was taken up into heaven. Before this, Jesus talked to the apostles He had chosen. With the help of the Holy Spirit, Jesus told them what they should do. After His death, He showed Himself to them and proved in many ways that He was alive.

The apostles saw Jesus during the forty days after He was raised from death. He spoke to them about the kingdom of God. Once when He was eating with them, He told them not to leave Jerusalem. He said, "The Father has made you a promise which I told you about before. Wait here to receive this promise. John baptized people with water, but in a few days you will be baptized with the Holy Spirit. . . . Then you will receive power. You will be My witnesses—in Jerusalem, in all of Judea, in Samaria, and in every part of the world."

After He said this, as they were watching, He was lifted up. A cloud hid Him from their sight. As He was going, they were looking into the sky. Suddenly, two men wearing white clothes stood beside them. They said, "Men of Galilee, why are you standing here looking into the sky? You saw Jesus taken away from you into heaven. He will come back in the same way you saw Him go."

—Acts 1:1–5, 8–11 ICB

Luke recounts that Jesus told them the Good News and what they should do with it. Jesus had help and the disciples would need help too. Who is that help? What did they need power to do?

...

A witness is a person who sees something take place. What did Jesus prove to the disciples after He died and before He ascended? What were they told to do with the proof?

...

When they witnessed something remarkable, men in white asked them why they were still standing there, looking into the sky. Could they have meant, "Don't just stand there! Do something"? Why?

LET'S DO

One of the best ways to share Jesus with others is to tell them personal stories of how God showed up in the lives of people you know. Have each family member write down their real-life God stories and remember to share them when the right time comes.

LET'S PRAY

Dear God, thank You for giving us proof. Help us be Your proof like the disciples were. In Jesus' name, amen.

84

SHARING THE LOVE

You and many others have heard what I have taught. You should teach the same thing to some people you can trust. Then they will be able to teach it to others.

—II Timothy 2:2 ICB

This teaching is true: If we died with Him, then we will also live with Him . . . If we say we don't know Him, then He will say He doesn't know us. If we are not faithful, He will still be faithful, because He must be true to who He is.

Continue teaching these things. And warn people before God not to argue about words. Arguing about words does not help anyone, and it ruins those who listen. Do the best you can to be the kind of person that God will approve, and give yourself to Him. Be a worker who is not ashamed of His work—a worker who uses the true teaching in the right way.

—II Timothy 2:11–15 ICB

We were made right with God by His grace. And God gave us the Spirit so that we could receive the life that never ends. That is what we hope for. This teaching is true. And I want you to be sure that the people understand these things. Then those who believe in God will be careful to use their lives for doing good. These things are good and will help all people.

—Titus 3:7–8 ICB

LET'S THINK

The Bible tells us the truth. What is the truth?
What should we do with that truth and why?

...

The Bible warns us to not argue about words. Why?
What should we be concerned about instead?

...

The Bible tells us many times how we are made right with God.
How can we be sure we understand "these things"?
How can "these things" we learn from the Bible help all people?

LET'S DO

What are some of your favorite Bible promises?
Have each family member come up with one truth
they are standing on today.

LET'S PRAY

Dear God, thank You for the truth found in Your written Word.
Help us learn it, do it, and teach it to others. We love You.
In Jesus' name, amen.

85

CALLING WHO?

The boy Samuel served the Lord under Eli. In those days the Lord did not speak directly to people very often. There were very few visions. Eli's eyes were so weak he was almost blind. One night he was lying in bed. Samuel was also in bed in the Lord's Holy Tent. The Ark of the Covenant was in the Holy Tent. God's lamp was still burning. Then the Lord called Samuel.

Samuel answered, "I am here!" He ran to Eli and said, "I am here. You called me."

But Eli said, "I didn't call you. Go back to bed." So Samuel went back to bed.

The Lord called again, "Samuel!"

Samuel again went to Eli and said, "I am here. You called me."

Again Eli said, "I didn't call you. Go back to bed."

Samuel did not yet know the Lord. The Lord had not spoken directly to him yet.

The Lord called Samuel for the third time. Samuel got up and went to Eli. He said, "I am here. You called me."

Then Eli realized the Lord was calling the boy. So he told Samuel, "Go to bed. If He calls you again, say, 'Speak, Lord. I am your servant, and I am listening.' " So Samuel went and lay down in bed.

The Lord came and stood there. He called as He had before. He said, "Samuel, Samuel!"

Samuel said, "Speak, Lord. I am your servant, and I am listening."

—1 Samuel 3:1–10 ICB

LET'S THINK

*Samuel heard—literally heard—God's voice calling him. He thought it
was the voice of the main priest in God's temple. Why did Samuel not
recognize God's voice? Would you recognize God's voice? Why?*

...

*Eli had made a lot of mistakes in his past; however, he finally realized
that God was calling Samuel and told the boy the right thing to do.
How does God use imperfect people to show us the truth?
What else does God use to get our attention?*

...

*Read those last lines of Scripture again.
Did you realize that God was standing there? Think about that!*

LET'S DO

*Praying is about listening too! Take time to be quiet and listen for
God's still small voice (1 Kings 19:11–12).*

LET'S PRAY

*Dear God, thank You for calling us. Help us hear Your voice and do
what You say. In Jesus' name, amen.*

TO DO WHAT?

So prepare your minds for service and have self-control. All your hope should be for the gift of grace that will be yours when Jesus Christ comes again. In the past you did not understand, so you did the evil things you wanted. But now you are children of God who obey. So do not live as you lived in the past. But be holy in all that you do, just as God is holy. God is the One who called you. It is written in the Scriptures: "You must be holy, because I am holy."

—I Peter 1:13–16 ICB

Jesus will keep you strong until the end. He will keep you strong, so that there will be no wrong in you on the day our Lord Jesus Christ comes again. God is faithful. He is the One who has called you to share life with His Son, Jesus Christ our Lord.

—I Corinthians 1:8–9 ICB

My friends, you must do all you can to show that God has really chosen and selected you. If you keep on doing this, you won't stumble and fall. Then our Lord and Savior Jesus Christ will give you a glorious welcome into His kingdom that will last forever.

—II Peter 1:10–11 CEV

LET'S THINK

*God has called us to do many things all for His purpose
(Romans 8:28). We need to be ready. How do we prepare our
minds? What service does He want us to do?*

•••

*We are to be different. How do we "be holy," "do no wrong,"
and "do all we can to show" it? What's the point of all this?
What do we hope for?*

•••

*Only Jesus is perfect, and God is faithful—what Jesus did for us on the
cross still counts. Why do you suppose we are still being challenged
to do the right things?*

LET'S DO

*Like we often do for the New Year, make a New Life's Resolution
instead. Have each family member share what they can do differently
to show that they are called to follow Jesus.*

LET'S PRAY

*Dear God, thank You for helping us stay on the right track and be
different than the world. Welcome us into Your heavenly kingdom.
In Jesus' name, amen.*

WHAT ELSE?

Jesus said to the followers, "Go everywhere in the world. Tell the Good News to everyone."

—*Mark 16:15 ICB*

God has brought you out of darkness into His marvelous light. Now you must tell all the wonderful things that He has done.

—*I Peter 2:9 CEV*

Always be ready to answer everyone who asks you to explain about the hope you have. But answer in a gentle way and with respect.

—*I Peter 3:15 ICB*

God chose you to be His people. I tell you now to live the way God's people should live. Always be humble and gentle. Be patient and accept each other with love.

—*Ephesians 4:1–2 ICB*

I'll tell you what it really means to worship the LORD. Remove the chains of prisoners who are chained unjustly. Free those who are abused! Share your food with everyone who is hungry; share your home with the poor and homeless. Give clothes to those in need; don't turn away your relatives.

—*Isaiah 58:6–7 CEV*

God has done marvelous things for us! We are commanded to tell the world. How are the first two verses similar yet different? What has God done that you can tell others about? Are you ready to explain the hope you have?

•••

Christians should live as God wants us to—like Christ. Think of recent examples that show Christlike humbleness, gentleness, patience, or love.

•••

Worship can be singing praises, but name some other ways we can worship the Lord too (see Isaiah 58:6–7).

LET'S DO

It's impossible to do all these things—and everything else in the Bible—perfectly. We try our best, and God helps us. He loves us despite our shortcomings. Share about a time when you saw someone doing the right thing.

•••

Just for fun: role play and tell each other about the hope you have. You could be yourself or switch roles and pretend to be each other!

LET'S PRAY

Dear God, help us be Your mouth, hands, and feet. Help us tell others, serve others, and love others as You want us to. In Jesus' name, amen.

STANDING STRONG

Keep alert. Be firm in your faith. Stay brave and strong.

—I Corinthians 16:13 CEV

You will be saved by being faithful to Me.

—Luke 21:19 CEV

If we are not faithful, He will still be faithful, because He must be true to who He is.

—II Timothy 2:13 ICB

Brothers, the Lord loves you. God chose you from the beginning to be saved. . . . You are saved by the Spirit that makes you holy and by your faith in the truth. God used the Good News that we preached to call you to be saved. He called you so that you can share in the glory of our Lord Jesus Christ. So, brothers, stand strong and continue to believe the teachings we gave you. . . . We pray that the Lord Jesus Christ Himself and God our Father will comfort you and strengthen you in every good thing you do and say. God loved us. Through His grace He gave us a good hope and comfort that continues forever.

—II Thessalonians 2:13–17 ICB

LET'S THINK

God loves us so much! Even when we fail, we know that God is faithful. Think of several reasons why we need to be reminded of this truth. When has He been faithful in your life?

...

When in battle, facing the enemy, we must be alert and standing our ground. God will strengthen us like He did David (#56; see I Samuel 17). He will also comfort us with the Holy Spirit, our Helper (#39; see John 14:26). Can you think of other biblical examples when someone needed God's comfort or strength? What about today? When would His help be needed?

LET'S DO

Share how you have been reminded to be faithful or God has reminded you that He is faithful.

LET'S PRAY

Dear God, thanks for being faithful even when we are not. Thanks for giving us the strength to follow You until the very end. We love You. In Jesus' name, amen.

89

CARRY ON

Praise the Lord! Thank the Lord because He is good. His love continues forever. No one can tell all the mighty things the Lord has done. No one can speak all His praise.

—*Psalm 106:1–2 ICB*

Lord, Your Word is everlasting. It continues forever in heaven. Your loyalty will continue from now on. You made the earth, and it still stands. All things continue to this day because of Your laws. All things serve you. If I had not loved Your teachings, I would have died from my sufferings. I will never forget Your orders because You have given me life by them. I am Yours. Save me.

—*Psalm 119:89–94 ICB*

But what the LORD has planned will stand forever. His thoughts never change.

—*Psalm 33:11 CEV*

Jesus Christ is the same yesterday, today, and forever.

—*Hebrews 13:8 ICB*

I will always sing about the Lord's love . . . I will say, "Your love continues forever. Your loyalty goes on and on like the sky."

—*Psalm 89:1–2 ICB*

LET'S THINK

God has done many amazing things! Let's think about some of them.
Can you remember a Bible story about. . .
God loving us? Hint: a short guy (#1) and ninety-nine sheep (#7).
Defying the laws of nature? Hint: a storm (#4), water (#43), oil
(#46), fire from heaven (#57), go fish! (#61), bread and fish (#62),
freed (#63), a god "bowed" down (#64). God's healing power:
Hint: not leopards (#40), no longer crippled (#44), no longer dead
(#45), seeing (#s 58–59), from a distance (#60).
The free gift? Hint: all throughout but especially the Best Gift (#54).

LET'S DO

Share about some things you learned by reading
and doing the prompts in this book.

•••

What were your favorite family moments through this process?

LET'S PRAY

Dear God, thanks for being true to Your Word forever and ever.
Thanks for Your never-ending love and being there for us
no matter what. In Jesus' name, amen.

90

TIME TO CELEBRATE

Then Jesus said, "A man had two sons. The younger son said to his father, 'Give me my share of the property.' So the father divided the property between his two sons. Then the younger son gathered up all that was his and left. He traveled far away to another country. There he wasted his money in foolish living . . .Soon after that. . .there was not enough food to eat anywhere in the country . . . So he got a job. . .to feed pigs. The son was so hungry that he was willing to eat the food the pigs were eating. But no one gave him anything. The son realized that he had been very foolish. He thought, 'All of my father's servants have plenty of food. But I am here, almost dying with hunger. I will leave and return to my father. I'll say to him: Father, I have sinned against God and against you. I am not good enough to be called your son. . . .' So the son left and went to his father.

"While the son was still a long way off, his father saw him coming. . . . [His father] ran to him, and hugged and kissed him. The son said, 'Father, I have sinned against God and against you. I am not good enough to be called your son.' But the father said to his servants, 'Hurry! Bring the best clothes and put them on him . . . Then we can have a feast and celebrate! My son was. . .lost, but now he is found!' So they began to celebrate.

—Luke 15:11–24 ICB

LET'S THINK

Perhaps the most amazing thing God has done is that
He knew we would mess up—and He died for us anyway.
Why do you think the father celebrated the son's return in the parable?

LET'S DO

Share with a heart full of celebration how much God loves us
and has a plan for us. Share how the Good News has
personally impacted you.

LET'S PRAY

Dear God, thanks for being true to Your Word, for loving us and
celebrating when we come Home! In Jesus' name, amen.

TAKE TEN!

TAKE TURNS LETTiNG EACH FAMiLY MEMBER ANSWER THE QUESTiONS BELOW.

About Others

1   How can we tell others about what God has done?

2   How can we use our unique talents to share God's love?

3   What makes a good teacher and why?

About You

4   How has God blessed you?

5 What is God calling you to do for Him?

6 What godly power would you like so you can share the Good News more easily with others?

About Stuff

7 What do you like to do to celebrate?

8 What is one of your favorite ways to worship God?

9 How can we keep that attitude of celebration for what God has done for us?

10 How can we hear God's voice when we pray?

LIVE YOUR FAITH

Dear Friend,

This book was prayerfully crafted with you, the reader, in mind. Every word, every sentence, every page was thoughtfully written, designed, and packaged to encourage you—right where you are this very moment. At DaySpring, our vision is to see every person experience the life-changing message of God's love. So, as we worked through rough drafts, design changes, edits, and details, we prayed for you to deeply experience His unfailing love, indescribable peace, and pure joy. It is our sincere hope that through these Truth-filled pages your heart will be blessed, knowing that God cares about you—your desires and disappointments, your challenges and dreams.

He knows. He cares. He loves you unconditionally.

BLESSINGS!
THE DAYSPRING BOOK TEAM

Additional copies of this book and other DaySpring titles can be purchased at fine retailers everywhere.
Order online at <u>dayspring.com</u>
or
by phone at 1-877-751-4347